LEADERSHIP FOR
SOCIAL JUSTICE
AND
DEMOCRACY
IN OUR SCHOOLS

The Soul of Educational Leadership

Alan M. Blankstein, Paul D. Houston,
Robert W. Cole, Editors

Volume 1: Engaging EVERY Learner

Volume 2: Out-of-the-Box Leadership

Volume 3: Sustaining Professional Learning Communities

Volume 4: Spirituality in Educational Leadership

Volume 5: Building Sustainable Leadership Capacity

Volume 6: Leaders as Communicators and Diplomats

Volume 7: Data-Enhanced Leadership

Volume 8: Leadership for Family and Community Involvement

Volume 9: Leadership for Social Justice and Democracy in Our
Schools

THE SOUL OF EDUCATIONAL LEADERSHIP

VOLUME 9

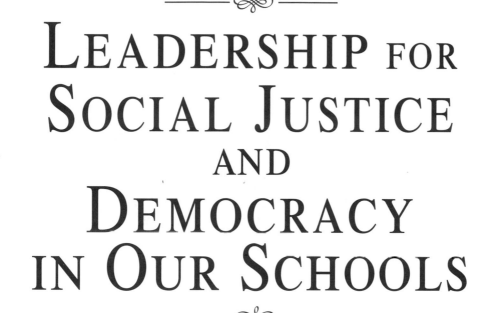

LEADERSHIP FOR SOCIAL JUSTICE AND DEMOCRACY IN OUR SCHOOLS

ALAN M. BLANKSTEIN ~ PAUL D. HOUSTON

EDITORS

A JOINT PUBLICATION

American Association of
School Administrators

CORWIN
A SAGE Company

FOR INFORMATION:

Corwin

A SAGE Company

2455 Teller Road

Thousand Oaks, California 91320

(800) 233-9936

Fax: (800) 417-2466

www.corwin.com

SAGE Ltd.

1 Oliver's Yard

55 City Road

London EC1Y 1SP

United Kingdom

SAGE India Pvt. Ltd.

B 1/I 1 Mohan Cooperative Industrial Area

Mathura Road, New Delhi 110 044

India

SAGE Asia-Pacific Pte. Ltd.

33 Pekin Street #02-01

Far East Square

Singapore 048763

Acquisitions Editor: Debra Stollenwerk

Associate Editor: Desirée A. Bartlett

Editorial Assistant: Kimberly Greenberg

Production Editor: Amy Schroller

Copy Editor: Teresa Herlinger

Typesetter: C&M Digitals (P) Ltd.

Proofreader: Victoria Reed-Castro

Indexer: Michael Ferreira

Cover Designer: Michael Dubowe

Permissions Editor: Adele Hutchinson

Copyright © 2011 by Alan M. Blankstein

Printed in the United States of America

Library of Congress Cataloging-in-Publication Data

Leadership for social justice and democracy in our schools / [edited by] Alan M. Blankstein and Paul D. Houston.

p. cm.—(The soul of educational leadership series ; 9)

"A joint publication with the Hope Foundation and the American Association of School Administrators."

Includes bibliographical references and index.

ISBN 978-1-4129-8161-3 (pbk.)

1. School management and organization. 2. Educational leadership. 3. Social justice. 4. Democracy and education. I. Blankstein, Alan M. II. Houston, Paul D. III. Hope Foundation. IV. American Association of School Administrators.

LB2805.L3433 2011 371.2—dc22 2010048885

This book is printed on acid-free paper.

11 12 13 14 15 10 9 8 7 6 5 4 3 2 1

CONTENTS

PREFACE

Reading through the titles of this series, The Soul of Educational Leadership, it seems as if they were all gearing up to this culminating volume: *Leadership for Social Justice and Democracy in Our Schools*. At the heart of engaging all learners (Volume 1), outstanding leadership (Volume 2), building a community of professionals (Volume 3), leading with spirit (Volume 4), building sustainable capacity (Volume 5), embracing a style of leadership that values communication and diplomacy (Volume 6), informing leadership strategies with sound data (Volume 7), and inviting families and the community into our schools lies a deep respect for and foundation in principles of social justice, fairness, equity, and democracy.

This last volume of the series explores how leaders might affirm and introduce democratic and socially just principles in our schools by reflecting on their own biases and assumptions, and then taking the necessary steps to transform these into prosocial behaviors that model socially just actions to their students and staff. The contributors to this volume address how socially responsible, proactive cultures in schools not only foster equity for students and staff alike, but also promote improved academic achievement for students who feel respected; valued as individuals with unique cultures, backgrounds, and needs; and motivated to share their assets with the school community.

We begin this volume with a chapter entitled "Respect" by Bonnie M. Davis, best-selling author and consultant on culturally proficient instruction to schools, districts, and professional organizations. Davis maintains that in order for there to be social justice in a community, participants must feel respected by one another. In an effort to encourage school leaders to understand the experiences and culture of others, Davis invites them to examine their own social position and underlying biases. As an example, she discusses her own background:

> We White people have unconscious knowledge of White middle-class culture's hidden rules; however, what is so familiar—White, middle-class codes of behavior or hidden rules—is hard to separate out and articulate to others. I find this true for many reasons, not the least of which is the fact that we often do not know our history and do not understand hierarchy, power, oppression, and the common attributes of the *isms*.

By beginning first to unpack our own positionality, we are in a better place to understand, and respect, how others might experience the world differently.

In Chapter 2, "Social Justice: Focusing on Assets to Overcome Barriers," the authors reiterate Davis's exhortation toward self-reflection so that leaders can begin to refashion school policies into those that are more equitable for all students. Randall B. Lindsey, Professor Emeritus at California State University, Los Angeles; Delores B. Lindsey, Associate Professor at California State University San Marcos; and Raymond D. Terrell, Assistant Dean for Diversity and Research at Miami University in Oxford, Ohio, affirm that "Educators must first seek to understand their own assumptions about those who are culturally different from them, and then explore how those assumptions are embedded into the policies and prevalent practices in their schools and school districts." They emphasize that implementing new, more democratic policies must be a conscious decision on the part of the school leader—one that is explicitly communicated to the entire school community.

Linda Skrla, Kathryn Bell McKenzie, and James Joseph Scheurich, authors of Chapter 3, "Becoming an Equity-Oriented Change Agent," are, respectively, Associate Dean for Research and P–16 Initiatives, Associate Professor of Educational Administration, and Department Head of Educational Administration in the Department of Educational Administration and Human Resource Development at Texas A&M University. They encourage school leaders to become equity-oriented change agents who focus on the assets of others and avoid demonization as well as initiate courageous conversations, and who demonstrate persistence, patience, and focus. In order to bring about more socially just policies, the authors insist that school leaders must question "the attitudes and assumptions of those applying the rules and procedures." They point out that although some aspects of policies "may not be inequitable in and of themselves . . . the result or effect may be inequitable."

Tackling the issue of unequal practices in hiring, C. Cryss Brunner and Yong-Lyun Kim in Chapter 4, "Are Women Prepared to Be School Superintendents? An Essay on the Myths and Misunderstandings," argue that decision makers need to reframe their perception regarding the types of experiences and training that are best suited to forming successful leaders in order to recognize the gifts of different types of leaders, particularly women, to lead districts in ways that promote instructional leadership, transformative leadership, and collaborative leadership to name a few. Unpacking and reframing misconceptions benefit not only one particular subjugated group, but the community as a whole. Brunner, Associate Professor at the University of Minnesota, and Kim, Assistant Professor at Hankuk University in Korea, write, "Some social justice scholars suggest that if discrimination against women and people of color was eliminated, their hiring would be one solution for the reported superintendent shortage, smaller applicant pools, and declining quality in candidate pools."

Once leaders have successfully questioned their own positionality and the inequalities in existing policies, they can begin to implement positive, more democratic practices in their schools. Marvin W. Berkowitz, Professor of Character Education and Codirector of the Center for Character and Citizenship at the University of Missouri-St. Louis, in Chapter 5, "Leading Schools of Character," provides numerous examples of leaders modeling the socially just attitudes and actions they would like their staff and students to adopt. Berkowitz insists that "the principal . . . is the centerpiece of character education's quality and success." He goes on to say, "For schools to become the kinds of moral and democratic institutions that promote the development of students, they need leaders who understand, prioritize, and have the leadership competencies to nurture such institutional growth."

Promoting schools of character and promoting social justice is a win–win situation all around. Positive school cultures will not only nurture social responsibility and a sense of equity in students, but they will also lead to increased student engagement and academic achievement. In Chapter 6, "Leading for Social Responsibility," Sheldon H. Berman, Superintendent of the Jefferson County Public Schools in Louisville, Kentucky, contributes the following:

> Too often, we are warned that if we take our eye off of reading and math to pay attention to social responsibility, we will see standardized test scores falter. In actuality, just the opposite occurs. Academic achievement is critically linked to school and classroom culture, to student engagement, and to students' sense of meaning in their studies.

Berman affirms not only the promise of improved academic achievement, but also, perhaps more importantly, a return to the value of nurturing socially responsible citizens who will become the leaders of tomorrow. He concludes,

> Preparing our children to assume a responsible role in the world will be critical to our nation's future welfare, for these young people are inheriting a world replete with significant environmental, political, and social issues. Their ability to discern injustice, understand the complexity of problems, and demonstrate commitment to civic participation is crucial to finding just solutions to those issues.

In the same vein as building schools of character and determinedly teaching social responsibility, Mara Sapon-Shevin in Chapter 7, "Zero Indifference and Teachable Moments: School Leadership for Diversity, Inclusion, and Justice," maintains that leaders need to implement a zero-indifference policy to bullying and discrimination in schools. Leaders should do so in such a way that rather than acting as bystanders to instances of bullying and social injustice, students learn to become multiculturally literate, to recognize discriminatory practices, and to act and speak out against the social injustices they encounter in their day-to-day lives. Sapon-Shevin, Professor of Inclusive Education at

Syracuse University, states that schools need to take an "activist stance" to establish "an inclusive, diverse school community." She says, "Our goal cannot be to mirror the injustices and inequities of the broader society (and world) but rather, to provide students with the skills, attitudes, and confidence they need in order to actively transform the world."

Finally, Paul D. Houston, president of the Center for Empowered Leadership (and an editor of this series), urges school leaders to model socially just and prosocial actions not only within the school itself, but also outward toward the larger community. In the closing chapter, "Getting Kids Ready for School—Raising the Village," Houston makes the point that if it takes a village to raise a child, then we have to first raise the village. "The first task of a school is to shoulder the burden of remaking the village. This is the only way real success is possible." Remaking the village must be a collaborative undertaking. Speaking as a school leader, he asserts,

> "My job isn't to heal the problems here. My job is to create the conditions so that the community can heal itself." School leaders must be in the "healership" business. That simply means, don't be the source of the conflict and work to allow the people who care most about the schools—the parents and community—to find ways to work together for the benefit of the children.

As we observed in previous volumes of this series, healthy, positive school cultures and democratic practices benefit not only the student body, but also the entire learning community, including, ideally, the community around the school. The authors of this volume have presented numerous models and examples of how leaders can implement more democratic practices and act in socially just ways so that students and staff will in time follow their lead and in turn act and implement socially responsible practices in their given roles. As Sapon-Shevin writes in this volume, "The lessons we teach our students—whether overtly and intentionally or mindlessly and inadvertently—are what will shape the world they live in."

ABOUT THE EDITORS

Alan M. Blankstein is Founder and President of the HOPE (Harnessing Optimism and Potential through Education) Foundation, a not-for-profit organization, the Honorary Chair of which is Nobel Prize–winner Archbishop Desmond Tutu. The HOPE Foundation is dedicated to supporting educational leaders over time in creating school cultures where failure is not an option for any student. Founded in 1989, the HOPE Foundation has focused for the past decade on helping districts build leadership capacity to close gaps and sustain student success.

The HOPE Foundation launched the professional learning communities movement in educational circles, first by bringing W. Edwards Deming and later Peter Senge to light in a series of Shaping America's Future forums and PBS video conferences from 1989 to 1992. The HOPE Foundation now provides some 20 conferences annually, highlighting their long-term successes in sustaining student achievement in districts and regions in 17 states and parts of Canada and South Africa.

A former "high risk" youth, Alan Blankstein began his career in education as a music teacher and has worked in youth-serving organizations since 1983, including the March of Dimes; Phi Delta Kappa; and the National Educational Service (now Solution Tree), which he founded in 1987 and directed for 12 years.

Author of the NSDC Book of the Year and best-seller *Failure Is Not an Option: 6 Principles for Making Student Success the ONLY Option,* Blankstein is also publisher of three *Failure Is Not an Option* video series. In addition, he coauthored the Reaching Today's Youth curriculum and has published articles in *Educational Leadership, The School Administrator, Executive Educator, High School Magazine, Reaching Today's Youth,* and *Inside the*

Workshop. He has also provided keynote presentations and workshops for virtually every major educational organization.

Alan Blankstein served on the Harvard International Principals Center's advisory board, as board member for Federation of Families for Children's Mental Health, as cochair of Indiana University's Neal Marshall Black Culture Center's Community Network, and as advisor to the Faculty and Staff for Student Excellence (FASE) mentoring program. He also served as advisory board member for the Forum on Race, Equity, and Human Understanding with the Monroe County Schools in Indiana and on the Board of Trustees for the Jewish Child Care Agency (JCCA), in which he was once a youth-in-residence.

Paul D. Houston served as executive director of the American Association of School Administrators (AASA) from 1994 to 2008. He is currently president of the Center for Empowered Leadership (CFEL). Dr. Houston has established himself as one of the leading spokespersons for American education through his extensive speaking engagements, published articles, and regular appearances on national radio and television.

Dr. Houston has coauthored three books: *Exploding the Myths,* with Joe Schneider; *The Board-Savvy Superintendent,* with Doug Eadie; and *The Spiritual Dimension of Leadership,* with Steven Sokolow. He has also authored four books: *Giving Wings to Children's Dreams: Making Our Schools Worthy of Our Children, Articles of Faith and Hope for Public Education, Outlooks and Perspectives on American Education,* and *No Challenge Left Behind: Transforming America's Schools Through Heart and Soul.*

Dr. Houston was previously a teacher and building administrator in North Carolina and New Jersey. He has also served as assistant superintendent in Birmingham, Alabama, and as superintendent of schools in Princeton, New Jersey; Tucson, Arizona; and Riverside, California.

Dr. Houston has also served in an adjunct capacity for the University of North Carolina, as well as Harvard, Brigham Young, and Princeton Universities. He has been a consultant and speaker throughout the United States and overseas, and he has published more than 200 articles in professional journals.

ABOUT THE CONTRIBUTORS

Marvin W. Berkowitz, PhD, is a developmental psychologist, and he is the inaugural Sanford N. McDonnell Professor of Character Education and codirector of the Center for Character and Citizenship at the University of Missouri-St. Louis. His areas of expertise are child and adolescent moral development, moral and character education, and educational leadership and reform. He is the editor of the *Journal of Research in Character Education,* and serves on the board of directors of the Character Education Partnership. He is the author of over 100 journal articles, book chapters, monographs, and books, including *Parenting for Good* (2005). In 2006, he received the Sanford N. McDonnell Lifetime Achievement Award from the Character Education Partnership.

Sheldon H. Berman, EdD, was appointed superintendent of the Jefferson County Public Schools (JCPS) in Louisville, Kentucky, in 2007, having previously served 14 years as the superintendent of the Hudson (MA) Public Schools. In JCPS (with over 99,000 students), Berman led the creation of a new student assignment plan that meets the standards of the U.S. Supreme Court, while sustaining the district's strong commitment to diversity and quality. He launched a districtwide program to build students' social skills; the creation of an elementary social studies curriculum; and a high school restructuring plan that includes freshman academies, trimester scheduling, and career-themed schools of study. In addition, he restructured staff to drive curricular reform and promote innovation, initiated curricular innovations in mathematics and science, and piloted a program to place nurses in the schools. Early in his career, he was a founder and president of Educators for Social Responsibility. He is the author of numerous articles, books, and chapters on civic education, character education, service-learning, virtual education, and education reform.

C. Cryss Brunner, PhD, is an associate professor at the University of Minnesota's Department of Organizational Leadership, Policy, and Development, and she has conducted research (on identity, power, superintendency, technology, and leadership preparation) appearing in more than 50 scholarly chapters, books, and articles. In addition to authoring one book and editing two books (one with Lars Björk), she recently coauthored the book *Women Leading School Systems: Uncommon Roads to Fulfillment* (2007) with Margaret Grogan. Brunner is a recipient of the National Academy of Education's Spencer Fellowship for work on superintendents, power, and decision making, and the 1998 University Council for Educational Administration (UCEA) Jack Culbertson Award for outstanding contributions as a junior professor. With Margaret Grogan, she was recognized in 2006 by the American Association of School Administrators for research on women superintendents. Additional awards include the University of Minnesota's Multicultural Teaching and Learning Lifetime Fellowship and others for her virtual power and identity-sensitizing process, Experiential Simulations.

Bonnie M. Davis, PhD, is a veteran teacher of more than 30 years who is passionate about education. She has taught in middle schools, high schools, universities, homeless shelters, and a men's prison. She is the recipient of numerous awards, including Teacher of the Year and the Governor's Award for Excellence in Teaching. She holds a PhD in English. Her publications include *How to Teach Students Who Don't Look Like You, How to Coach Teachers Who Don't Think Like You,* and *The Biracial and Multiracial Student Experience: A Journey to Racial Literacy.* Davis has presented at numerous national conferences and provides services to schools through her consulting firm, Educating for Change.

Yong-Lyun Kim, PhD, is an assistant professor at Hankuk University of Foreign Studies in Seoul, Korea. He earned his PhD in the Department of Educational Policy and Administration at the University of Minnesota, Twin Cities. He teaches courses about research methodology and leadership practice and theory. His research interests include school leadership, gender equity, policy analysis, and program evaluation for leadership effectiveness. His research appears in journals such as the *Journal of Educational Administration* and the *Journal of Research on Leadership Education.*

Delores B. Lindsey, PhD, is associate professor of educational administration at California State University, San Marcos in California. She is coauthor of four Corwin publications: *Culturally Proficient Learning Communities: Confronting Inequities Through Collaborative Curiosity* (2009), *Culturally Proficient Instruction: A Guide for People Who Teach* (2002, 2006), the multimedia kit by the same name, and *Culturally Proficient Coaching: Supporting Educators to Create Equitable Schools* (2007). Lindsey is a former middle grades and high school teacher, middle grades site administrator, and county office of education administrator. As a professor, she serves schools, districts, and county offices as a cognitive coach training associate, an adaptive schools associate, and a consultant to develop culturally proficient educators.

Randall B. Lindsey, PhD, is professor emeritus at California State University, Los Angeles, where he served as chair of the Division of Administration and Counseling in the School of Education. He has served as a junior and senior high school teacher of history and as an administrator of school desegregation and staff development programs. He has worked extensively with school districts as they plan for and experience changing populations. He also served as interim dean of the School of Education at California Lutheran University and is principal associate with the Robins Group. It is his belief and view that too often White people are observers of issues related to diversity, equity, and access, and to that end, the focus of his writing and work with schools involves being accountable for the education of all children and youth.

Kathryn Bell McKenzie, PhD, is an associate professor in the Department of Educational Administration and Human Resource

Development at Texas A&M University in College Station. Her research foci include equity and social justice in schools, school leadership, qualitative methodology, and critical White studies. During her over 20 years in public education, she has been a classroom teacher, curriculum specialist, assistant principal, and principal.

Mara Sapon-Shevin, PhD, is Professor of Inclusive Education at Syracuse University where she prepares teachers for inclusive education and social justice teaching. Her areas of interest and expertise include full inclusion; anti-oppressive education; using music, movement, and theater to teach for social justice, cooperative learning, and anti-bullying education. She works frequently with school districts who are seeking to address issues of diversity in a more proactive and inclusive way. She has also served as an expert witness in lawsuits related to inclusive education. Sapon-Shevin is the author of over 150 books, chapters, and articles. Her most recent books include *Widening the Circle: The Power of Inclusive Classrooms* (2007) and the just-published second edition of *Because We Can Change the World: A Practical Guide to Building Cooperative, Inclusive Classroom Communities* (2010).

James Joseph Scheurich, PhD, is professor and head of the Department of Educational Administration and Human Resource Development at Texas A&M University. His research interests include equity in education, schools and districts that are successful with diverse students, race and racism, educational accountability, and qualitative research methodologies. He is the editor of a research journal, serves on the editorial boards of several others, has written over 35 journal articles, and has published five books. He has served on several committees for national research organizations and is currently on the Executive Committee for the University Council for Educational Administration (UCEA). In 2006, he received the UCEA Master Professor Award for helping prepare so many successful young professors in his research field, and he was a 2008 nominee for president of the American Educational Research Association (AERA).

Linda Skrla, PhD, is a professor of educational administration and the associate dean for research and P–16 initiatives in the College of Education and Human Development at Texas A&M University. She holds a PhD from the University of Texas at Austin and has extensive experience as a public school teacher and administrator. Her research focuses on equity issues in school leadership and policy, including accountability, highly successful school districts, and women superintendents. Her work has appeared in numerous journals, and she has coauthored or coedited four other books, including *Leadership for Equity and Excellence: Creating High-Achievement Classrooms, Schools, and Districts* (2003); and *Accountability and Equity: Policies, Paradigms, and Politics* (2003).

Raymond D. Terrell, EdD, is the assistant dean for diversity and research in the School of Education, Health, and Society and is an associate professor in the Department of Educational Leadership at Miami University in Oxford, Ohio. He has served as an elementary school principal in Hamilton, Ohio, after retiring as a professor of educational administration and dean of California State University's School of Education. He began his career as a public school teacher and administrator and has more than 30 years of professional experience with diversity and equity issues.

CHAPTER ONE

RESPECT

BONNIE M. DAVIS

Michael mouths off to Mrs. Martin, the teacher, when she asks him to move to another desk and stop talking to his classmates. She sends him to the office. The assistant principal asks Michael why he talked back to Mrs. Martin. He replies, "She disrespected me." The assistant principal meets Mrs. Martin at the door to her classroom and asks, "What happened between you and Michael?" Mrs. Martin replies, "Michael didn't respect me."

What does respect look like to the 16-year-old African American male in our classrooms? What does respect look like to an older White female teacher? How are these two human beings alike and how do they differ? What causes them to hold differing definitions of respect? And why are they unaware of each other's definition? If they understood what respect "looked like" to each other, would this situation have evolved into its inevitable miscommunication? In other words, what we know about each other usually supports our communication, and *what we don't know we don't know* too often severs our ability to find a common definition of respect and create classrooms for optimal learning. Too often we find the word *respect* posted on school walls with no explicit teaching, learning, or understanding of what it means to the students of different cultures sitting in classrooms. Respect embodies a cultural worldview, and when we educators *do not know what we don't know* about the meaning of respect and what it means to *all*

1

—————— ✂ ——————

Respect embodies a cultural worldview, and when we educators do not know what we don't know about the meaning of respect and what it means to all of our students, we face a huge disadvantage. The meaning of the word respect changes according to those defining it.

of our students, we face a huge disadvantage. The meaning of the word *respect* changes according to those defining it.

Michael's daily journey in life is both like and unlike Mrs. Martin's journey. He defines respect in both similar and dissimilar ways. Their positive communications and their possible conflicts arise out of their understanding and their mis-understanding of what respect looks like to each other. Mrs. Martin may define respect as the student remaining quiet while she lectures. Michael may define respect as not being called out in front of his peers and embarrassed with the demand that he move to another seat. Each feels wronged and disrespected. If, instead, Mrs. Martin and Michael understood each other's definitions of respect, they might have avoided the situation. Had they understood each other, they would have been practicing *intercultural competence*. Intercultural competence is the ability to successfully interact with people of other cultures. Since Mrs. Martin and Michael seemingly lacked that ability in this instance, their inability to interact across cultures is an example of *intercultural entanglement*. Intercultural entanglement occurs when people of different cultures become embroiled in a situation due to a lack of understanding of the other's culture, or the hidden codes or rules of that culture. In this case, the cultures being misunder-stood may be White and Black—or adult and adolescent; nonethe-less, two *individuals* misunderstood the hidden rules held by each other and perceive each other as lacking in respect and being cultur-ally insensitive. Hidden rules are the unspoken codes of expected behavior in a given situation. Violating these hidden codes, or rules, can show disrespect toward another. How do we learn what respect looks like to each of us, and how do we learn to respect, honor, and feel empathy for one another? This is one of the many challenges we face as educational leaders who strive to create spaces and places of social justice and democracy in our classrooms.

When we apply it to the classroom, social justice means equal access to opportunity. Since social justice is based on equality or equal opportunity for all students in our classrooms, we must ask, "What is and what is not equal opportunity?" In addition, as educational leaders we continue journeys along entangled pathways to social justice by challenging ourselves to learn, respect, and honor *what we don't know we don't know about each other and about ourselves.*

As a staff developer and teacher-leader, I ask these questions: How do I respect and honor the journey of individual educators while expanding their understanding of what they *don't know they don't know* and can learn about themselves and their students and colleagues? How can I support the development of empathetic understanding for others in both my own mind and in the minds of others? How can we learn what it feels like to walk in another's shoes? How do I continue to grow in awareness, expand my knowledge base, and continue my journey? The *interracial model of mutual respect* (Figure 1.1) illustrates the journey.

Figure 1.1 Interracial Model of Mutual Respect

As shown in Figure 1.1, this framework consists of four broad categories broken down into several subcategories. The four areas of growth are (1) looking inside ourselves, (2) listening to and learning from others, (3) integrating new knowledge, and (4) a call to action. These categories, or stages, are cyclical and recursive. The growth unfolds in ways that overlap and cycle back. This chapter briefly examines each of these as a framework for the journey to learn *what we don't know we don't know* and how to respect and honor the journey of every individual.

LOOKING INSIDE OURSELVES

Our personal experiences comprise the cultural lens through which we perceive the world. People often ask me how I, a White woman, became interested in race. The catalyst for my journey began on my 30th birthday when I met a Black man who became my husband and the father of my son.

Leaving the Deep South after completing graduate school, I settled in St. Louis in an all-White school district and taught for 17 years before a "voluntary" desegregation order brought one small busload of Black students from the inner city of St. Louis to the outer suburban school district where I taught. These students largely remained invisible the first year they attended the high school where I taught, and I had none of the students in my upper-level English classes. Yet the teachers felt I was the one who should know what to do with "those" students since eight years earlier I had met, fallen in love with, and married a Black man, subsequently having a biracial baby; thus, in their eyes, I was the "expert" on race in the building.

Since others felt I was the expert on race and due to personal interest, I began to study issues of race seriously in the early 1980s, doing my dissertation on oppression within the literary canon. In the mid-1980s, I began my foray into staff development in this arena. Now, decades later, I question what are the optimal pathways to increase understanding of racial issues in our schools? How might we best support White teachers who enter classrooms filled with few or many students who don't look like them, teachers who wonder if they need to do anything differently? These might be

- Teachers who wonder if they *need* to do something different, and if so, then how might they do it;
- Teachers who wonder what this all has to do with their Whiteness;
- Teachers who, perhaps, do not understand the necessity of acknowledging their Whiteness and who need tools to deconstruct the subject of White culture;
- Teachers who need tools to examine White female or male culture as it impacts their classroom management and instruction;
- Teachers who do *not* want to address any of this—who say they do not see "color" and they treat all children the same;
- Teachers who believe they are good people (and they are) and who don't see the need to bring up these difficult topics;
- Teachers who don't accept the non-closure of dealing with issues of race and teachers who don't want to participate in discussions surrounding race;
- White teachers who don't want to believe that raw racial discrimination still exists for their colleagues of color, or for their colleagues with whom they do not interact but assume they understand their realities and experiences;
- Teachers who just can't believe the stories they hear from people of color and who ask, "When did this happen?" refusing to believe this is the present—not the past;
- Teachers who have had limited experience with people from other cultures and find it difficult to develop empathy for them.

Yes, discrimination still occurs. I fight daily my racist biases. In workshops, I offer examples of my own thoughts—call them racist or biased or stereotypical, but they are thoughts I continue to fight. For example, while working out on a treadmill in a hotel in Omaha, Nebraska, I noticed a woman who appeared about my age walk by with cleaning supplies, clearly a woman who was there to clean rooms. Looking at her, I thought, "I can't believe this woman is still cleaning toilets at my age [64], and she's even White!" When I ask participants in workshops to discuss what they had just heard, they say things such as, "It's classist because you don't think cleaning toilets is as honorable a job as what you do." They say, "It's sexist because you don't think women should be the ones cleaning toilets." And they say, "It's racist because you assume only women of color are the ones who clean toilets in hotel rooms."

We discuss all of these assumptions, and I share with them that I believe I would not have *noticed* that woman had she been a woman of color. I believe I would have gone on watching the morning news on the television set overhead. But because I had to confront my assumption when I saw an older, White cleaning woman, I was able to reflect upon my stereotypical, classist, sexist, racist bias. Then I ask myself, "How does this subconscious belief carry over into the classroom where I teach or into the workshop or into my daily interaction with other human beings?" I continually challenge myself: When a White man walks into the room with a woman of color, do I assume the man is the superintendent and the woman of color is a principal? Do I continue to assume the person of authority is the White person, no matter what the situation? Various people of color I have spoken with tell me this happens to them often. They are automatically assumed by others to hold the less prestigious position. Can I explain this away by referring to my past and the number of incidents that reaffirm my expectations and my biases? How do we talk about this with each other? And when we do, how do we communicate showing respect and honoring the journey of each individual involved yet move the conversation along the path to social justice?

Moving along the path to social justice is challenging. And what does that even mean? I believe the abstractness of the definitions of terms such as *respect* and *social justice* contribute to the challenge. These terms are abstract and may hold different meanings for different individuals. I won't understand the definitions you hold for these words unless you give me concrete examples of how respect and incidences of social justice play out in your world. So why not have students and faculties do just that? Why not hold courageous conversations in our educational settings—with protocols for communication—allowing students and educators to share with each other their definitions of respect, their definitions of social justice, and their definitions of empathy?

"How does this subconscious belief carry over into the classroom where I teach or into the workshop or into my daily interaction with other human beings?"

An important way to respect the journey of each individual is to *hear* each other's stories or journeys. When we share our story and others truly *listen without judgment,* we communicate more deeply and understand more fully. Another powerful tool is to read the literature of the cultures of the students in our classrooms. As a former English teacher, I learned the power of literature to create a shared understanding and develop empathy and respect for others.

None of this is easy. Our journeys involve pain, transparency, cognitive dissonance, self-disclosure, vulnerability, and reflection. The journey also demands we drop the mantle of defensiveness and adopt a childlike innocence and wonder, as well as a readiness to learn *what we don't know we don't know.* What does it mean when *we don't know we don't know* something? Here is an illustration: Recently I presented to a staff in North Carolina who were teaching a new student population: Karen students, a group of ethnic peoples from Myanmar. I had never heard of this population. I didn't know the location of the students' country or even its name, what language the students spoke, or how to identify them among the other students. In other words, *I didn't know I didn't know there was a group of people called Karen.* I am not stupid, yet I did not know about these people. So *what we don't know we don't know* doesn't mean we're stupid; it means we are ignorant of information about others or about ourselves. This happens in every arena. Some educators may be insensitive to their colleagues' needs and to student needs because they don't know they don't know. I may be insensitive to others' needs because I don't know I don't know. This brings us back to the same question: How can we respect and honor the journey of every educator and every student? How can we acknowledge the experiences of each of us while continuing to learn what we don't know we don't know about the *other?*

When I began my journey to understand culture and race, I was ignorant of the magnitude of the task. When I ask teachers to articulate White middle-class culture's hidden rules or codes, things become murky. They find it difficult to state the underlying expectations we hold for behaviors in a White middle-class culture, even though most of us educators are White and middle class. We White people have unconscious knowledge of White middle-class culture's hidden rules; however, what is so familiar—White middle-class codes of behavior or hidden rules—is hard to separate out and articulate to others. I find this true for many reasons, not the least of which is the fact that we often do not know our history and do not understand hierarchy, power, oppression, and the common attributes of the *isms*. Many educators have not been taught how White women have been socialized in this country, and since the majority of teachers are White women, we often do not understand how this socialization plays out in our classrooms in our communications with students and colleagues, the forms of classroom management we apply, and our hesitancy to be direct and clear in some situations. My study of White women's communication patterns—reading the works of Carol Gilligan, Becky Bailey, Deborah Tannen, and others—greatly informed me and supported my understanding of how and why cultural entanglement occurs so frequently in our classrooms.

Most of my workshop participants are White and have never thought about what it means to be White, or if the fact of their Whiteness impacts their relationships with their students or the academic achievement of their students of color.

Most of my workshop participants are White and have never thought about what it means to be White, or if the fact of their Whiteness impacts their relationships with their students or the academic achievement of their students of color.

When my book, *The Biracial and Multiracial Student Experience: A Journey to Racial Literacy,* was released in June of 2009, I expected general audiences of educators to be interested in the book due to the growth in the number of multiracial students in their schools and because of President Obama being elected, which had triggered an increased awareness of race in the United States. Instead, educators who express interest are mostly those who have multiracial children or grandchildren of their own. It is their personal, real-life experience that connects them to the book, not the presence of multiracial students in their schools or the political climate of the country. This is a normal human reaction. We respond to things that interest us and are a part of our own personal human experience. If we do not have firsthand multiracial experience, then why and how would we know there are things we do not know about that experience or even that it *is* a different experience? This further emphasizes the necessity of connecting new learning to one's own personal experience and affirms the necessity of connecting learning to the lives of the students sitting in our classrooms. In other words, we often are not interested in things that do not connect to our lives, yet we expect students to want to learn about topics that hold no interest for them. However, we can develop an interest by building a classroom community through doing the following:

- Discussing abstract concepts like respect and social justice, allowing students and staff an opportunity to share personal stories and connections to the terms
- Reading the literature from cultures other than our own
- Sharing personal narratives with our peers
- Having students do oral histories of their families and others in their communities
- Inviting people from the community into the school to share their stories
- Practicing listening without judgment to the narratives of others

LISTENING TO AND LEARNING FROM OTHERS

Writing a book on the multiracial experience was a way for me to deepen my understanding about race. I listened to the stories of 40 individuals who self-identified as people of color, biracial, multiracial, White, or other. It was an entry point for my having a much broader discussion about race and racial identity and how it affects students in our schools. Granted, a thorough discussion of race must include the history of the systematic oppression of groups of people, but such a discussion is beyond the scope of this chapter. However, unless we frame the work of social justice in a larger picture than that of individual discrimination, we weaken our ability to bring about systemic change. All of us have suffered individual discrimination. You may have been discriminated against due to your gender, your body image, your sexual identity, your visible or invisible disability, your ethnicity, your religion, your class, your demographics, or other issues. However, the discussion in this chapter focuses on discrimination resulting from skin color prejudice or racial identity.

The work begins within us through listening to our own thoughts. The work expands as we listen and learn from others.

One powerful exercise is to quietly listen to another's story. If we attempt to listen without judgment, we open ourselves to hearing the story. Below are three stories: The first is a description of a "day" in my life; the second is a description of a "day" in Dorothy's life, my close friend (when Dorothy and I are in public with my son, people usually assume Dorothy is my son's mother); and the third is a narrative written by my son contemplating his racial identity (he is biracial, White and African American).

A Day in My Life:
Bonnie M. Davis, Educational Consultant

I awake. I read the paper and watch the television news where I see White men portrayed as the authority, full of confidence, with a vocal style that matches mine. My speaking patterns are reinforced—they refer to their mothers as "Mother" or "Mom," not "Mama" or "Mum." Their vocabulary, even their accent, matches my middle-class White, midwestern self. I drive to work.

Mostly I pass Whites driving cars as I drive from a suburb up a superhighway that stretches through the middle of St. Louis to the University of Missouri. I see passengers of my own color in the majority of the cars.

At the building where I work, there are approximately 25 people. Four are African American women, three of whom are support personnel. None is Asian. None is a Black male. None is Hispanic. It is reinforced throughout my day that my culture is in charge, correct, and successful.

After work, I drive to a fitness center where I work out. Usually one or two African Americans work out there, too, but the interesting thing is that all of the cleaning people and the service people in the coffee shop are Black. The only Black person in the spa section is the receptionist, a light-skinned woman with long, flowing hair. I see that Blacks clean the toilets at the fitness center; Whites and one Asian do the massages and manicures.

I drive home to a neighborhood block that is 80% White. There are a few neighbors who are people of color. One biracial woman is married to a White male; others are Asian and Hispanic. One is a Black male.

I watch the 5:00 PM news. The anchors are White; the important news usually revolves around Whites, usually males. Stories
of violence mostly depict Blacks.

My friends are mostly middle-class White women like me.
My significant other is a White male. I don't have to worry
about being followed by security at the local shopping mall; I
don't have to worry about being stopped by the police because
of my skin color. I don't have to worry about being invisible
in my community. I am acknowledged when I walk up to a
counter, whether it is a fast-food place, the cleaners, the video
counter, or the local school.

I am White. I have unearned power because of my skin color.

Source: From B. Davis, *How to Teach Students Who Don't Look Like You: Culturally Relevant
Teaching Strategies.* Corwin, 2006, p. 56. Reprinted with permission.

A Day in My Life: Dorothy J. Kelly,
Director of Desegregation/Assistant Principal

In this "White" or "dominant culture" society, I feel like I
wear my Blackness as an offense to some people. I do not have
just one typical day, because for me the days are a continuum of
responses to race and racism. I do not have any protection against
what I may encounter—I simply have the wisdom of a warrior.

When I wake up, I view the news and hear what seems to be
endless accounts of Black-on-Black crime. I see sad mug shots of
Black folk, mostly males, and always there is commentary from
a family member or bystander. I often cringe, hoping not to hear
the name of a former student or one of their family members. I
have recognized several over the past 20 years.

Despite how my day starts, I manage to make it to the neighborhood coffee shop, pick up coffee, and drive to work pretty
happy about what I might encounter. Although I live in an integrated community, I rarely see any people of color at the coffee
shop, not any Asians, Latinos/as, or African Americans—just
White baristas and customers. Currently, my workplace has 14
people of color: 12 African Americans and 2 Chinese. The remaining 100 employees are White. I am one of two African American
administrators in the school district. Previously, I worked as the
first and only African American administrator for over 10 years,

and I was the single African American employee in my building for the duration of my tenure with the district. I now work with (in my opinion) an ethnically diverse staff.

I am challenged on personal and professional levels by issues of race and racism. The challenges do not happen every day, but I have been challenged so many times that there is no doubt to me and to whoever is privy to the "onslaught" that it is indeed about my being African American and it is undeniably about race or racism. My decisions may be questioned or second-guessed by the staff members whom I supervise. My ideas sometimes seem to be dismissed or not perceived as legitimate explanations surrounding matters of African American student achievement by my fellow administrators. White parents comfortably insult Black students or me by using racial slurs and blatant stereotypes when discussing matters of conflict between their child and a student of color or teacher of color. In turn, Black parents comfortably challenge my racial identity or Blackness when they disagree with a decision I have made about their son or daughter who is involved in a conflict with a White student or White teacher.

Another insult that I occasionally encounter is that I'm called "nigger" by a White parent who is angry. I have encountered racial slurs numerous times: "nigger," "Black bitch," "jiggaboo," "you're just one of them." Equally disturbing, I'm also called some of these racial slurs by African American parents. I have been told by an angry White parent after I suspended her son for fighting that the KKK is watching how I treat White kids. I have been told by a White teacher that I would not be allowed to observe her or I would be sued. I have been told by a White teacher that I better not come into her room or she would report me to the board of education. I have been jokingly told by a White teacher that when the desegregation program started, she had to take down a sign in her room that said, "No administrators and no niggers allowed." While sitting with a group of Black employees at my current job, I have been teased by a White teacher that we are planning a conspiracy together, yet White teachers sit together all the time without fear of being alluded to as conspirators. As an administrator, I try to be professional, friendly, and respectful to everyone. I walk a balance beam because of my supervisory role, and I have to hold back on a personal level because by being a Black supervisor, you are always in fear of being removed from your job. This is a common belief among African American administrators or supervisors in most fields. You have an uneasy feeling that others, especially White people, believe you were hired because you are Black, and you fear you will be fired (laid off, phased out, downsized) because you are Black. I also find in talking with other African Americans that we get the "Black" problems whether they are one of our students or not. And no one wants to admit to that particular phenomenon.

The best encounters during my days are with the students. At times it is hard for students to put their feelings of discrimination into words—they just know they were treated unfairly. A teacher may scold them for disruptive behaviors that White students are not reprimanded for by the same White teacher. They may fail classes even though they have completed all the assignments and received passing grades on all those assignments but fail or achieve low test scores. They cannot find any other explanation for the F, nor can their parents. African American students and other students of color complain of racism when a White teacher or a White student makes a racially insensitive remark or joke and no one intervenes. I understand that I'm working with middle school students, and their sense of fairness is skewed at times, but I also understand when issues of race or racism are present. In turn, I understand that many White teachers are uncomfortable, untrained, and unable to talk about matters of race and racism.

My day as an African American runs on a continuum to the degree that I encounter race and racism—not because it's one day, one morning, or one afternoon; it is ongoing day after day and year after year. Even in my personal life, I have endured humiliating racial incidents such as not getting served in a restaurant or standing at a counter for several minutes when a White male or female butts in front of me and gets immediate service. I can be smartly dressed or casually dressed and I'm somehow still invisible. It makes me wonder who really is ignoring me, the person who butts in front of me or the service person who is supposed to be waiting on me. Perhaps the worst is when, for some unknown reason, a White person will drive by and holler out a racial slur at me—I can only pray that a physical attack does not take place next. Sometimes I keep track of this by marking the date it occurred, but eventually I get discouraged, and I think to myself, Don't keep a record of racism, because it only increases the tension and stress that goes with being a Black person.

As my day ends and as I mature in my career, I appreciate the drive home and entering the safe place where I can momentarily think of things that are not about race and racism.

Source: From B. Davis, *How to Teach Students Who Don't Look Like You: Culturally Relevant Teaching Strategies.* Corwin, 2006, pp. 57–59. Reprinted with permission.

A Day in My Life: R. Davis, Mixed, African American/White, Born 1979, Career Professional

I guess I don't think about it too, too much. I've been considered Black basically my whole life, so it's something I've learned to adapt to. I'm guessing that is a common trait to all mixed people of any ethnicity or race—adapting. You learn to be Black enough to be part of one category and White enough to be part of another (if that's what your mixture is). If you ask if this makes one schizophrenic, I would say no, just smarter and provides a good ability to improvise. This is not a new concept or strange whatsoever. Your average Black or Latino is probably used to acting one way in the corporate world versus how they would act in the real world amongst friends and family.

And then the term mixed. What the hell does that mean? If you are half Irish and half Cuban, what are you? And why do certain groups of people get labeled that and others don't? For example—Black, White, Puerto-Rican, Asian. . . . Most Puerto Ricans are in fact of mixed heritage, but for some reason, their ethnicity is on par with other people's race. Why is that? If you look at a census form, many say Hispanic and are lined up among other racial categories. So could you not be a White Puerto Rican? And if you claim you are Hispanic, and your ancestors are from Spain, are Spanish people from Spain not considered Anglo Saxon or White like most other European groups?

Why even get lost in all that madness of labels? Most mixed people would say the best you can do is to be you because many people won't understand that you fall outside of the categories . . . seems to be a foreign concept to them. Maybe it's for simplicity sake. Yes, I would say I'm Black because I won't get quizzed on what my background is. And there's not always a lot of time to sit down and discuss this topic every time someone asks you, nor should you have to.

I'm not going to lie; I honestly think trying to find some commonality among other mixed people is a little bit of a lost cause. Interesting, yes, but I am going to see you as a person and not our common bond as being mixed. This is because I am almost sure the way you grew up and your background is different from mine. I think a lot of mixed people attempt to break down their background in order to better explain themselves to the world. ("Oh, my dad is German and Italian, and my mother is Haitian and Native American.) If I do this, it's out of interest of my background, but not so I can spew a long explanation at someone when asked, "What is your background?" Not remembering exactly what the question was (but the topic was race), my Black friend once told me, "No, you're a nigga," as if to verify my racial category. I think that's pretty solid evidence of what I am physically perceived as, wouldn't you agree?

Overall, I would say I like it. I can get along or be accepted by almost anyone, and there are many places around the heterogeneous world where I blend right in. The challenge is being able to keep up the act. For example, I basically look like a light-skinned African American man. I bet I could go to a place, like say, Morocco, and blend in relatively well. However, my Arabic skills are nonexistent, and my French is only passing. So maybe I would fit in if I were mute—but anyway, the moral is I think most mixed people would say it is an undeniably positive feeling to be around people who look like you and blend in. This is an experience that I felt in Brazil, a feeling of belonging, but guess what? I only speak "um puoco" of Portuguese, and people growing up there would have a completely different story growing up than I, so how do we relate?

The negative is that there is never complete satisfaction of belonging. You're a drifter, a gray space, a neutral color, not loud enough to offend anyone either which way.

Source: From B. Davis, *The Biracial and Multiracial Student Experience: A Journey to Racial Literacy,* Corwin, 2009, pp. 6–7. Reprinted with permission.

After reading these narratives, consider the following questions:

- What differences do you find in Bonnie's day, Dorothy's day, and R. Davis's day?
- What responsibilities do you have to learn about the experiences that people from other cultures confront daily?

- What responsibility do you have to examine your own privilege in every decision that is made in your educational setting?
- What responsibility do you have to examine the privilege of White children in every decision that is made in your educational setting?
- What are some ways you can make yourself accountable for privileging all children?
- If you are a person of the dominant culture, can you call attention to oversights, conscious or unconscious, in order to be self-accountable?

Source: From B. Davis, *How to Teach Students Who Don't Look Like You: Culturally Relevant Teaching Strategies.* Corwin, 2006, pp. 59–61. Reprinted with permission.

Listening to the stories of others allows us to expand our thinking. These three stories cannot be generalized to represent all White women, all African American women, and all multiracial individuals, yet they offer descriptions of lives on which I can reflect and which I can deconstruct (including my own). When I read Dorothy's story, I note the invisibility she describes, and I think about the dismissive indifference of the dominant culture when people butt in front of her in line or ignore her at the counter of a store. I think of my own patterns of behavior. Do I dismiss others? Do I butt into conversations, interrupting the speaker? Do I judge behavior as I listen, or do I listen without judgment, seeking to understand, respect, and honor another's experience that differs from my own? I hear stories of invisibility again and again from people of color in my workshops. It is a common theme and recited too often to be an anomaly. I learn from these stories of invisibility that I must respect and honor others by acknowledging each individual's humanity.

I look for patterns of stereotypical thinking. Do I automatically assume the person of color was hired because of his or her color? Can I admit I do that? Do I assume to know a person and make judgments on their worth or ability by the way they look? Do I assume that stories like mine are the stories of those who have worked hard and that those stories carry no privilege? Do I understand what it means to be a White woman educator in this system? Am I able to deconstruct the invisible mantle of my privilege and dig into the history of systematic oppression of groups to understand the systemic institutionalized racism that pervades our educational system? Do I stand up or stand back?

INTEGRATING NEW KNOWLEDGE BY CONNECTING TO THE LIVES OF STUDENTS

Creating Social Justice Through Equal Access to Content Knowledge

This spring I spent 6 weeks observing and coaching 30 teachers in nine high schools in an urban, northern California school district, part of an equity project focused on supporting teachers as they implemented classroom strategies to culturally connect to students' lives. I watched these teachers working hard to connect with a variety of student cultures: adolescent, gender, ethnic, class, gang, or others. The most successful teachers were those who knew their subject matter and consistently, carefully, and considerately connected the academic content to their students' lives through examples, stories, metaphors, analogies, and interactive activities. Whether the discipline was physics, history, biology, English, Spanish, or math, the content they taught had to be relevant to the students' lives in order to engage them. This was not easy.

As I observed these teachers, I wondered the following:

1. Do the teachers really know what the students' lives are like? Have they driven by the homes of the students or visited families in their homes?

2. Do they understand the roles that institutions—churches and community organizations—play in the lives of the students?

3. Do they know and understand the gang culture and how it affects their students? Do they understand other peer cultures of their students?

4. Do the teachers understand the brain research to know the importance of making the connections from the content material to students' lives, and can they articulate that to their students? These are high school students, so why not share with them this information about how the brain works?

5. Do the teachers know and understand their content well enough—to the point of automaticity—to be able to think metaphorically and make connections to students' lives?

6. Do the teachers work in a climate where they can share ideas and formulate ways to make important connections for their students to their content?

If teachers can answer "yes" to most of the above, they have a greater opportunity for creating an equitable classroom where respect is practiced by each individual in the room.

What needs to happen in a classroom? The following is an example in which I observed a teacher who put into practice his knowledge of his students and his content area.

I sit in a classroom in an urban high school. I am here to observe and coach teachers. I look around at all Black and brown students. I observe teachers, Black, brown, White. (Over the past several days, I found classrooms ranging from students totally engaged with the work to classrooms where students were off task and doing nothing but talking—or nothing at all. Fortunately, in most classrooms I found students engaged in the learning.) This morning I observe a history teacher who has asked for feedback on his transitions between topics and how he builds relationships with students through using the instructional material. He begins his class with a quiet, calm statement. He is dressed in a suit and tie, his daily uniform. (He tells me he is one of the few Latino teachers in the building and knows he is a role model.) He tells the students exactly what they will be learning that day (the standard is also posted clearly on the board) and requires they repeat it back to him in a choral fashion. He uses a warm-up that ties directly to the concepts he intends to teach. He uses nonverbal signals throughout the class; he uses humor appropriately; he is playful but serious; the students stay engaged. I observe him getting a male student to move from a back seat to a front seat without stopping his instruction, then engaging the student. I am impressed. His classroom is filled with visuals of role models from a variety of cultures as well as charts, student pictures, sports information, and other visuals that relate to the students. He integrates student movement flawlessly into the room filled with 42 bodies. He does mini-lectures, peppering his lecture with personal references to his students' lives and throwing in a few Spanish words and phrases. He uses analogies to student lives to illustrate his major points. He has students process the information and share with others. He salvaged old white tiles to use as response boards for his students so he can continually check for understanding. He includes a creative activity to deepen the understanding of the material. He concludes with "check-out" slips to monitor understanding.

The following are some practices I observed:

- The teacher tells the students exactly what they will be learning that day.
- The warm-up ties directly to the lesson.
- The teacher uses humor appropriately.
- The teacher uses a pair/share discussion of the material.
- The teacher uses a visual timer for discussion, reflection, and other work.
- The teacher uses graphic organizers.
- The teacher uses nonverbal commands.
- The teacher uses direct verbal commands.
- The teacher uses innovative materials.
- The teacher uses proximity.
- The teacher connects to students' lives with the content.
- The teacher holds high expectations.
- The teacher has outstanding classroom management.
- The teacher has students working with others.
- The teacher has students working at higher levels, ending with a creative activity to embed the learning.

Several students I interviewed said this teacher was their favorite. It was easy to see why. Respect oozed from him. His classroom was quiet and respectful even though the school was situated in an area known for its gangs and violence. After class, I asked students what they liked about the class and the teacher. Below are two responses from students in this teacher's class.

Mr. G. is a great teacher because he understands us all. He knows where we need help. He teaches us like he was one of us. There might be a lot of people in this class, but he always seems to have time for every single one of us if we need help. You got to respect us if you want to receive it.

"Mr. G. is a great teacher because he understands us all. . . . He teaches us like he was one of us. There might be a lot of people in this class, but he always seems to have time for every single one of us if we need help. You got to respect us if you want to receive it."

Mr. G. is a great teacher. He helps students where they are in need of help. He always has a positive attitude and always respects the students. Most teachers don't understand that. Mr. G. understands that you have to have a good attitude and respect to receive it from the students.

One of the highlights of this experience was the opportunity to interview students and ask their opinions about their teachers and their schools. Time and time again, the students stated that they liked a teacher when the teacher demanded they do the work and helped them when they needed help. Finally, they almost always brought up the R-word: Respect.

This in no way is a comprehensive description of best practices; however, it is a small vignette of powerful strategies teachers can use to show respect and honor for their students. Our students are the future, and unless we can understand what respect means to them and show them that respect, we diminish our ability as effective teachers who support all students to achieve at high levels.

CALL TO ACTION

Student eyes light up when they discover the stories of others, when they feel empathy and respect for the characters in literature. I remember one summer when I was teaching an English class in a community college. Many of the women students came out of poverty and held housekeeping jobs in local motels. They had never read about the plights of women throughout the world and by being introduced to this literature, they were incensed and ready to take action. In their essays, they expressed empathy for these women characters to whom they could relate; they learned from their stories.

In Martin Luther King's *Letter From a Birmingham Jail,* he writes about the necessity for taking action. "Human progress never rolls in on wheels of inevitability," writes King, refuting those who believe that time heals all and inevitably brings change. This attitude, he writes, stems from "the strangely irrational notion that there is something in the very flow of time that will inevitably cure all ills. Actually, time itself is neutral; it can be used either destructively or constructively." Dr. King's words are a call to action: In order to use time constructively, we must make a conscious decision to change. "Change is a conscious decision," writes Leonard Pitts, Jr., in *Change Is the Result of Choice, Action* (2010), published in the *Miami Herald*.

How do we do support change? We know classrooms are changing; however, the classroom leaders—the teachers—are not changing. White women make up the vast majority of classroom teachers in the United States. White women generally expect students to adhere to middle-class White norms and expectations. The browning of school classrooms explodes with cultures outside the dominant group and begs for White teachers to find out *what we don't know we don't know* about students who don't look like us. The complexity of the cultures comprising our classrooms challenges all of us.

Those of us who are White teachers can work to educate ourselves and change what we can. We can

- Investigate our racial history;
- Answer reflective questions about the work;
- Learn what we don't know we don't know about the experiences of others;
- Listen nonjudgmentally to the stories of others and consider the perspectives of others;
- Integrate the new knowledge we learn into our classroom practices;
- Encourage our students and our colleagues;
- Respect and celebrate the differences among our students and colleagues.

The work doesn't end. It is ongoing. It happens every day when we monitor our thoughts and actions. We can be vigilant in our schools. We can examine patterns of inequity. We can put our school practices under a giant microscope and look for institutionalized racism. It might appear in one of these forms as it did in my career:

- A counselor in an elementary school who believes that not all the students in Grades K–5 are capable of going to college

- A high school teacher who is so anxious to track students into ninth-grade English classes that break down racially, ensuring that the majority of Asian and White students end up in classes without Black and brown students except for the one exception that allows the teacher to justify the tracking
- A teacher who decides the books taught to students in the honors English classes are too difficult for the lower-track students and instead gives these students abridged and watered-down copies of Shakespeare and the classics
- A coordinator of gifted education who relies solely on indicators that limits inclusion of students of color
- The teachers who use only pedagogy that reinforces White culture and neglects the strengths of other cultures in the classroom
- The administration that refrains from posting visuals of role models of the cultures of the students represented in the schools as well as other cultures
- The receptionists who are rude to parents of color
- The curriculum committee whose members overlook the needs of each population in the school and rely heavily on the status quo

These practices are detrimental to our educational system; however, the most egregious practices are the ones I practice myself, since that is the one person I can change.

In self-assessing, consider asking the following:

Do we educators make transparent our prejudicial thoughts and biases? Do we examine our classroom practices for those who institutionalize racism and inequality? Do we examine our cultural lens and understand how our lens differs from others'? Do we question our ideology to ensure we are doing everything we can to halt the perpetuation of inequity? Do we have an understanding of what respect looks like to all those with whom we interact? Do we engage in practices that support intercultural competence?

The most egregious practices are the ones I practice myself, since that is the one person I can change.

Learning to respect others is not a cliché or simple platitude. It is a necessary action if we are going to evolve as a society. When we do a better job of listening, respecting, and honoring each individual's story, we open ourselves up to developing empathy. This understanding illuminates how our entangled journeys bind all of us within one race—the human race.

REFERENCES AND FURTHER READING

Anderson, K. (2010). *Culturally considerate counseling: Helping without bias.* Thousand Oaks, CA: Corwin.

Bailey, B. (2000). *Conscious discipline: 7 basic skills for brain smart classroom management.* Oviedo, FL: Loving Guidance.

Davis, B. (2006). *How to teach students who don't look like you: Culturally relevant teaching strategies.* Thousand Oaks, CA: Corwin.

Davis, B. (2009). *The biracial and multiracial student experience: A journey to racial literacy.* Thousand Oaks, CA: Corwin.

Gilligan, C. (1982). *In a different voice.* Cambridge, MA: Harvard University Press.

Lindsey, R. B., Robins, K. N., & Terrell, R. D. (2003). *Cultural proficiency: A manual for school leaders.* Thousand Oaks, CA: Corwin.

Pitts, L., Jr. (2010, April 24). Change is the result of choice, action. *Miami Herald.* Retrieved November 4, 2010, from http://www .miamiherald.com/2010/04/24/1595394/change-is-the-result-of-choice.html

Schreck, M. K. (2009). *Transformers: Creative teachers for the 21st Century.* Thousand Oaks, CA: Corwin.

Singleton, G., & Linton, C. (2006). *Courageous conversations about race.* Thousand Oaks, CA: Corwin.

Tannen, D. (1990). *You just don't understand: Men and women in conversation.* New York: Ballantine.

CHAPTER TWO

SOCIAL JUSTICE

Focusing on Assets to Overcome Barriers

RANDALL B. LINDSEY,
DELORES B. LINDSEY, AND
RAYMOND D. TERRELL

Do we have the will to educate all children?

—Hilliard, 1991

The emergence of the term *social justice* over the past few years in schools of education and, increasingly, in P–12 schools reminds us of the prevalence of the phrase "all children can learn" that peppered so many schools' mission and vision statements a generation ago. The words and phrases seem to have been more rhetoric than reality. As promising as those words were, they didn't seem to inform policy or practice in a way that benefited all students. As we prepared this chapter, our research led us to an article by Connie North (2008) in which her 2006 ERIC and Amazon .com searches revealed approximately 320 published works and over 1,800 book titles using the term *social justice*. Her article illustrates the broad and deep discussion potential the term holds for educational community members who are serious about aligning actions with equity within a social context. The purpose of this chapter is to navigate through the shoals of trite usage of catchphrases and discuss *cultural proficiency* as a lens that educators use to improve their individual and organizational practices.

AUTHORS' PERSPECTIVE

We, the authors of this chapter, have served as elementary, junior high, and senior high school teachers. We have served as school administrators in the capacity of assistant principals, principals, and district office administrators. We began our educational careers in the 1960s and 1970s when school desegregation was the vehicle to address issues of social inequities. The perspective on issues of social justice discussed in this chapter has been framed by our experiences and our commitment to expanding the foundational democratic principles of the United States in ways that apply to all citizens. Our journey as educators in applying democratic principles to educational practice has been a journey in pursuit of social justice.

SOCIAL JUSTICE—
A CATCHPHRASE OR A COMMITMENT?

North (2008) introduced the term *catchphrase* in her incisive article "What Is All This Talk About 'Social Justice'? Mapping the Terrain of Education's Latest Catchphrase." As lifelong advocates for educational issues related to diversity, equity, and inclusion, we have noted, often with dismay, the many words and phrases used to tangentially confront barriers to providing appropriate and adequate education to historically marginalized students. Common language that too often accompanies social interventions as varied as desegregation and the many attempts at school reform employs "catchphrases" such as the following:

- All students can learn
- World-class education
- Students at risk
- Alternative schools

- Restructured schools
- Turnaround schools

In this chapter, we summarize what we have learned about social justice, both from the literature and from our experiences. From this summary of identifying social justice in terms of students' access to learning, we describe *cultural proficiency* as a social justice approach that focuses on our practice as educators, not on perceived deficiencies of the students and communities we serve. Our attraction to cultural proficiency is that it requires little investment beyond what our late colleague Asa Hilliard (1991) aptly described a half generation ago as the "will" to educate all children.

What Cultural Proficiency Is and Is Not

Cultural proficiency is a systemic and systematic way to address social inequities. Cultural proficiency is *not* an off-the-shelf program that treats culture as an exotic system of practices to be learned or avoided. Cultural proficiency is best described as

- A lens for viewing and experiencing the world;
- An approach for embracing similarity and difference;
- The way in which we interact and react to those who are culturally different from ourselves;
- A way in which we live 24/7 (as opposed to the manner in which we behave while at school);
- The embedding of the tools of this lens or approach into our professional practice as educators;
- A responsibility for addressing social disparities that foster inequities in our schools in a manner that successfully addresses unequal access and outcomes.

That students from all racial, ethnic, social class, ableness, cultural, and gender groups can learn at high levels is now beyond

That students from all racial, ethnic, social class, ableness, cultural, and gender groups can learn at high levels is now beyond dispute. What is at play now is the extent to which we educators are committed to learning how to educate children and youth from diverse cultural backgrounds.

dispute. What is at play now is the extent to which we educators are committed to learning how to educate children and youth from diverse cultural backgrounds. We begin this discussion by developing a rationale for "a socially just approach to education" and by describing *educator* and *social justice* as key terms.

Why Social Justice?

As curious citizens of the United States, we recognize that the phenomenon now known as the *achievement gap* has its roots in historical social inequities that are as much the foundation of this country as are the democratic principles of which our country is so rightly proud. We believe educators must understand that decades of intentional and consequential discrimination based on race, gender, ethnicity, social class, and ableness is the foundation for the disparities we face in society and our schools today. Concomitantly, we must recognize that the society that created and fostered these disparities also provided us with the tools to alleviate discrimination and to address inequities. At the federal, state, and local levels of government, systems of laws have made it possible to challenge and overturn legal forms of segregation and discrimination. That same system of laws is now being used to address the social inequity known as the achievement gap.[1] The path toward closing the achievement gap has not been an easy journey, but it is a journey yielding positive results and revealing intractable struggles. As public school educators, we are part of that system of laws that seeks to address the vestiges of systemic discrimination that has left the achievement gap as its legacy.

Key Term—Educator

We use the term *educator* to demonstrate the interdependence of teachers, counselors, administrators, staff members, and trustees and school board members. It is our experience that many efforts to close achievement gaps focus narrowly on changing teacher behavior or in developing principals as instructional leaders. While either approach may have merit, focusing on the role of teachers or site administrators without taking into account the people they work with too often leads to divisiveness and isolation. Educator is used as an inclusive term to communicate the interdependence of our roles as teachers, school leaders, and policy makers. As an inclusive term, educator denotes that the work of cultural proficiency is systemic in nature—both for the individual educator and the school or school district.

Key Term—Social Justice

Our operational definition of *social justice* is "doing what is right for our students." As you can see, our definition is nothing fancy or involved, just a straightforward commitment to educating children and youth. "Doing what is right," of course, has several antecedents that North (2008) has described well. In her review of the literature on social justice, North analyzed the tensions and contradictions posed among competing models of social justice, specifically "recognition" and "redistribution." She describes "recognition" as cultural groups competing for respect and dignity and "redistribution" as socioeconomic classes demanding equitable sharing of wealth and power. Both sets of issues from the larger society play out in schools.

Recognition, as described by North, is reflected in cultural proficiency's core standard of valuing diversity (see Table 2.1) and in the need for educators to provide a formal and hidden curriculum that reflects at least the cultural groups in the school. The concept of *redistribution* is recognized as the barrier of privilege and entitlement, the obverse of systems of oppression. The mere presence of systemic oppression in our society in the form of racism, sexism, and classism among other forms of oppression means that when some people lose rights and privileges due to the maintenance of those systems, others benefit, often unknowingly and unwittingly, from those same systems. The accountability movement has gained steam in the past decade and has clearly revealed disparities identifying who is well served by our current educational system and who is not.

From North's analysis, we selected key points that are consistent with our use of the four tools of cultural proficiency (see Table 2.1) and that readily relate to roles of educational leaders:

- Holding a value for education as a "right" that results in "engaging and satisfying learning" and "potentially satisfying work" (Lynch & Baker, 2005, cited in North, 2008, p. 11)
- Recognizing that singular approaches will not produce desired results

- Knowing that policy formulation approaches to creating socially just schools must involve those marginalized by current practice
- Implementing prevalent practices that respect and include multiple opportunities for educators, students, and parents/guardians "to experience diverse perspectives and people on a daily basis and to dialogue critically about difference, human rights, and social justice" (North, 2008, p. 5)
- Understanding that appreciating and respecting difference is not the same as tolerance. For difference to be appreciated and respected, shared principles must be explicit.
- Understanding that today's social and educational inequities are the product of historical and transnational forces that have benefitted some cultural groups while simultaneously marginalizing others based on their social class, racial, ethnic, gender, sexual orientation, or ableness memberships
- Creating systems of involvement for students that empowers them to create their own futures at the local, national, and international levels
- Developing a deep understanding of the relationship of systemic oppression (e.g., racism and sexism) to systemic privilege and entitlement as barriers to closing achievement gaps. An illustration is that systemic school reform is slowed because those who benefit from current practices don't see a need to change and assume the changes to be made are for those who are targets of systemic oppression.
- Recognizing that educators must first seek to understand their own assumptions about those who are culturally different from them, and then explore how those assumptions are embedded into the policies and prevalent practices in their schools and school districts

CONCEPTUAL FRAMEWORK OF CULTURAL PROFICIENCY[2]

Table 2.1, The Conceptual Framework for Culturally Proficient Practices, portrays the four tools of cultural proficiency (the barriers, the guiding principles, the continuum, and the essential elements) and the interrelationship of the tools. Take a moment to scan the table, and then read the prompts below to guide your reading and thinking.

Table 2.1   The Conceptual Framework for Culturally Proficient Practices

The Five Essential Elements of Cultural Competence

Serve as standards for personal, professional values and behaviors, as well as organizational policies and practices:

- Assessing cultural knowledge
- Valuing diversity
- Managing the dynamics of difference
- Adapting to diversity
- Institutionalizing cultural knowledge

The Cultural Proficiency Continuum portrays people and organizations who possess the knowledge, skills, and moral bearing to distinguish among healthy and unhealthy practices as represented by different worldviews:

Unhealthy Practices:	Differing Worldviews	*Healthy Practices:*

Unhealthy Practices:

- Cultural destructiveness
- Cultural incapacity
- Cultural blindness

Differing Worldviews

Healthy Practices:

- Cultural precompetence
- Cultural competence
- Cultural proficiency

Resolving the tension to do what is socially just within our diverse society leads people and organizations to view selves in terms unhealthy and healthy.

Barriers to Cultural Proficiency	E t h i c a l T e n s i o n	**Guiding Principles of Cultural Proficiency**

Barriers to Cultural Proficiency

Serve as personal, professional, and institutional impediments to moral and just service to a diverse society by

- being resistant to change,
- being unaware of the need to adapt,
- not acknowledging systemic oppression, and
- benefiting from a sense of privilege and entitlement.

Guiding Principles of Cultural Proficiency

Provide a moral framework for conducting one's self and organization in an ethical fashion by believing the following:

- Culture is a predominant force in society.
- People are served in varying degrees by the dominant culture.
- People have individual and group identities.
- Diversity within cultures is vast and significant.
- Each cultural group has unique cultural needs.
- The best of both worlds enhances the capacity of all.
- The family, as defined by each culture, is the primary system of support in the education of children.
- School systems must recognize that marginalized populations have to be at least bicultural and that this status creates a distinct set of issues to which the system must be equipped to respond.
- Inherent in cross-cultural interactions are dynamics that must be acknowledged, adjusted to, and accepted.

We suggest you read the table from bottom to top. From Lindsey, Nuri Robins, and Terrell (2009), we adapted the following prompts as guides for analyzing and understanding the conceptual framework:

- First, direct your attention to the bottom of the table and notice the manner in which the arrow flowing from the "Barriers to Cultural Proficiency" informs the left side of the continuum and, in effect, fosters unhealthy practices that are culturally destructive, incapacitating, and blind.
- Then, notice how the arrow flowing from the "Guiding Principles of Cultural Proficiency" informs the right side of the continuum, leading to healthy practices that are culturally precompetent, competent, and proficient. Adherence to the guiding principles as core values enables people and organizations to overcome personal and organizational barriers to cultural proficiency.
- For those on the right side of the continuum, the "Five Essential Elements" serve as standards for educator and school practices, enabling cross-cultural effectiveness.

UNDERSTANDING OUR VALUES, BELIEFS, AND ASSUMPTIONS IS FOUNDATIONAL[3]

Creating conditions that foster socially just educational opportunities and outcomes for our students requires our willingness to first examine our own assumptions and values and, second, to identify the assumptions and values that serve as the basis for our school or school district's policies and practices.

Creating conditions that foster socially just educational opportunities and outcomes for our students requires our willingness to first examine our own assumptions and values and, second, to identify the assumptions and values that serve as the basis for our school or school district's policies and practices. We have at our disposal two familiar communications techniques that support this exploration—reflection and dialogue.

- We define *reflection* as the conversation we have with ourselves to understand the how and why of our actions. How often do you, during your drive home after a day at school, think of the comments or decisions you have made and wonder to yourself, *If I had to do this over again, how might I do it differently?* Assuming you avoid the temptation to rationalize, you may be engaging in a level of reflection.

- We define *dialogue* as the conversation we have with others in seeking to understand the how and why of the values of colleagues, parents/guardians, and students that underlie their behaviors, values, or practices. It is our experience that true dialogue is fairly rare in most schools, whether P–12 or college/university. Too often, argumentation and debate are presented as dialogue. While argumentation and debate may be fundamental to creating common missions and visions in some settings, dialogue displays keen interest in others and is an asset when working across the cultural lines of race, social class, ethnicity, gender, sexual orientation, ableness, and faith. Yes, it takes precious time to learn and engage in dialogue, and when performed skillfully it yields the opportunity to forge common goals that serve diverse communities in ways they want and need to be served.

As you read the nine questions and the brief discussions that follow, begin to think about how you might engage your skills of reflection and dialogue. The first step is yours: Read each question and discussion; then, take time to *reflect* on your personal responses. Ask yourself, *What is my truthful, honest response to each question, and how do I react to the comments that follow each one?* Educational leaders who are willing to look deep within themselves to examine *why* and *how* they developed certain attitudes and values are well prepared to lead schools serving diverse communities.

The second step involves your role as school leader—at the county, district, or site level. We encourage you to engage with your colleagues in dialogue to surface deeply held assumptions and reach shared understanding of what "closing the learning gap" means to the school community. Inclusive dialogue sessions can yield carefully crafted statements that emerge to inform everyone in your school community of your shared beliefs and values about all students learning.

Nine Key Questions for Reflection and Dialogue

The nine questions that follow are designed as guides for individual educators and school districts to probe and understand their core values in working with communities that have populations with cultural characteristics different from their own. The purpose of these questions and comments is to provide the opportunity for reflection and dialogue that responds to the epigraph at the opening of this article—*Do we have the will to educate all children?*

Question 1. To what extent do you honor culture as a natural and normal part of the community you serve?

No Child Left Behind (2002) and Race to the Top (American Recovery and Reinvestment Act, 2009), along with countless state-level measures, have brought us face-to-face with the under-education of cultural demographic groups in ways that we have never before seen in the United States. Though the disparities have always been present, we now have the opportunity to discuss student learning in terms of race, ethnicity, gender, ableness, and language learning. As educators, we and our school district organizations must recognize the extent to which we regard these, and other cultural groupings, as asset-rich resources upon which to build our educational programs, not as accountability inconveniences, deficits, or sources of problems.

Question 2. To what extent do you recognize and understand the differential and historical treatment accorded to those least well served in our schools?

The disparities that we have come to acknowledge as the achievement or learning gap are often the product of our history. Though we may not have been party to intentional practices of segregation, racism, sexism, ethnocentrism, or any other form of oppression, it is our collective responsibility to recognize the historical and current bases of discrimination and assume responsibility for rectifying and correcting past injustices through socially just actions now. Initiating socially just actions begins with recognizing how many of us today have privileges earned by being members of dominant groups. Responsibility for change must begin with those of us in the education community and the manner in which we see the achievement/learning gap as *our* issue.

Question 3. When working with people whose culture is different from yours, to what extent do you see the person as both an individual and as a member of a cultural group?

We estimate that all of us like to be seen and valued for who we are. We may enjoy being part of a team that achieves; however, our group identity does not detract from also wanting to be appreciated for who we are as a person. Yet, when working in cross-cultural venues, some educators too often revert to use of terms such as *they* and *them* when referencing people from cultural groups different from themselves. At best, this often gives rise to the "model minority syndrome" that occurs when one member of the dominated group learns the cultural norms of the dominant group, and at worst leads to pitting one cultural group against another and asking *Why can't you be like* _____ *(the other group)* or other forms of scapegoating.

Question 4. To what extent do you recognize and value the differences within the cultural communities you serve?

The cultural groups in our schools are no more monoliths than are we who belong to the professional cultural group known as "educators." All of the cultural groups we serve have vast differences in education, incomes, faith practices, and lifestyles. The cultural groups in our school communities are as diverse as the broader community. The socioeconomic differences within cultural groups often give rise to groups having more similar worldviews across socioeconomic lines than they do within cultural groups.

Question 5. To what extent do you know and respect the unique needs of cultural groups in the community you serve?

A one-size-fits-all approach to education may serve the needs of schools at the expense of our students and their communities. Even within schools that have students conform to grooming standards and physical accommodations, those same schools have learned to acknowledge in their curriculum and in their teaching different learning styles, different cognitive styles, and the different ways people process information. The inclusive educator teaches and encourages colleagues to make the necessary adaptations in how schools provide educational service so that all people have access to the same benefits and privileges as members of the dominant group in society.

Question 6. To what extent do you know how cultural groups in your community define family and the manner in which family serves as the primary system of support for students?

Prevalent educational practice has been to assume that parents and other family caregivers who really care about the education of their children will avail themselves of opportunities to interact with the school. Increasingly, our schools have become adept at finding culturally inclusive ways of engaging parents and caregivers in support of student achievement.

We find that, too often, educators and parents have different perceptions of the term *parent participation.* Lawson (quoted in Lindsey, Nuri Robins, & Terrell, 2009) used the terms *communitycentric* and *schoolcentric* to describe these contrasting perceptions.

- *Communitycentric.* "Parents involved in activities that meet the basic needs of their children as going to school well fed, rested, and clean."
- *Schoolcentric.* "Parents involved in activities that are structured and defined for parents by schools." (p. 105)

Effective and meaningful partnerships between parents and schools require sensitive, respectful, and caring school leaders willing to learn the positive nature and culture of the community as well as identify barriers that have impeded progress in school–community relations. Two California schools, Tahoe Elementary School in Sacramento and San Marcos Elementary School in San Marcos, have identified their core values about parent/guardian involvement and have been successful in engaging parents in productive ways through school-site, home, and other off-site meetings.

The traditional, often stereotypic, image of Euro-American homes with a family identified as one mother, one father, and the children is now recognized as a limited view of "family." Today, culturally proficient school leaders acknowledge single-parent families, multiple-generation extended families, same-gender parents, foster care homes, and residential care homes as "family." Whatever the configuration for the children in our schools, their family is their family.

Question 7. To what extent do you recognize and understand the bicultural reality for cultural groups historically not well served in our schools?

Parents/guardians and their children have to be fluent in the communication patterns of the school as well as the communication patterns that exist in their communities. They also have to know the cultural norms and expectations of schools, which may conflict or be different from those in their communities, their countries of origin, or their cultural groups. In ideal conditions, their children are developing bicultural skills, learning to "code switch" to meet the cultural expectations of their environments. However, parents may not have these skills for adapting to new and different environments. Parents or guardians and their children are then penalized because they do not respond to the norms set by educators, because they do not navigate well the educational systems of the public schools.

Question 8. To what extent do you recognize your role in acknowledging, adjusting to, and accepting cross-cultural interactions as necessary social and communications dynamics?

We have encountered few educators who fail to recognize the historical and current impact of racism and other forms of oppression on current school environments. It is also our experience that our educator colleagues who do recognize and understand the huge toll that oppression takes, also understand how people who are *not* affected by those same systems benefit in unwitting ways. It is precisely the awareness of the dynamic nature of oppression versus entitlement that enables such educators to be effective in responding to the educational needs of cultural groups within their schools/districts.

Unless one has experienced intentional or unintentional acts of discrimination or oppression, a person cannot fathom the toll it takes on one's day-to-day life. The overrepresentation of students of color in special education programs and their underrepresentation in advanced placement and gifted and talented programs is not new information. Educators who are aware of such dynamics employ strategies and tactics that engage parents as partners in beneficial placements for their children.

Question 9. To what extent do you incorporate cultural knowledge into educational practices and policy making?

Experienced educational leaders recognize the need to learn the culture of a new organization. Their very survival depends on appropriate responses to cultural norms of the school community. Effective educational leaders, in addition, are aware of their own cultures and the impact their culture has on their school/district. Knowledge about school culture, our individual cultures, and the cultures of our community rarely arrives at our desktops in a three-ring notebook or a PDF file. Cultural knowledge is possessed by those who are keenly aware of themselves, their community surroundings, and the legacies and challenges experienced by cultural groups in the United States and local communities.

Educational leaders who possess this self-awareness and are effective in cross-cultural settings avoid phrases such as, *Doesn't everyone know that . . .?* or *I would hope parents see that as their responsibility,* or *It's the way we do things here, and they will have to adjust.* Phrases such as these marginalize outsiders and serve to perpetuate an "us against them" mentality.

Culturally proficient leaders share their own cultural knowledge, engage with the community, and invite community experts, knowing that such actions, over time, will lead to appropriately institutionalizing cultural knowledge. Such leaders recognize that reculturing schools to be responsive to diverse constituencies is an internal and intentional process.

Culturally proficient leaders share their own cultural knowledge, engage with the community, and invite community experts, knowing that such actions . . . will lead to appropriately institutionalizing cultural knowledge . . . Reculturing schools to be responsive to diverse constituencies is an internal and intentional process.

Responses to these nine questions can be the basis for guiding principles, or core values, that inform and support culturally proficient leadership. The principles help frame and focus the behaviors of teachers and school leaders intentionally on all students learning at levels higher than ever before.

USE INTERNAL ASSETS AND BE INTENTIONAL—ESSENTIAL ELEMENTS

As educational leaders, the learning gaps are ours to rectify. Shifting the culture of a school district from responding to learning gaps as compliance issues to responding in ways that transform organizational culture, relies on school leaders' uses of their internal assets of reflection and dialogue. This intentionality is a two-phase process of personal reflection and purposeful dialogue with colleagues. Response to these nine questions provides the basis for developing mission statements and core values intended to serve a diverse community. To be effective today, school leaders need strong core personal and organizational values (Collins & Porras, 1997; Lindsey et al., 2009; Senge et al., 2000). In addition to the values leaders currently hold, the values of cultural proficiency explicit in the nine guiding principles can serve as the foundation on which to reculture and transform schools and districts.

With an understanding of one's own values and assumptions and at least an emerging awareness of how assumptions about cultural groups are embedded in current policies and practices, we turn to the Five Essential Elements of Cultural Competence. The essential elements are used as standards to guide personal values and behaviors as well as school and district policies and practices. Table 2.2 portrays the essential elements as proactive statements to guide learning about the diverse communities we serve. Take a moment and read the five statements. Note how each statement is congruent with current assessment and accountability initiatives that hold us responsible for the education of all demographics and cultural groups of students in our communities.

Table 2.2   Five Essential Elements of Cultural Competence

- **Assessing Cultural Knowledge.** Learning about the community you serve, about how educators and the school as a whole react to the community you serve, and what you need to do to be effective in low-income and impoverished communities. Also, leading for learning about the school and its grade levels and departments as cultural entities in responding to the educational needs of the community

(Continued)

Table 2.2 (Continued)

- **Valuing Diversity.** Creating informal and formal decision-making groups inclusive of parents/guardians and community members whose viewpoints and experiences are different from yours and those of the dominant group at the school, and that will enrich conversations, decision making, and problem solving

- **Managing the Dynamics of Difference.** Modeling problem solving and conflict resolution strategies as a natural and normal process within the culture of the schools and the socioeconomic contexts of the communities of your school

- **Adapting to Diversity.** Learning about socioeconomic and cultural groups different from your own and the ability to use others' experiences and backgrounds in all school settings

- **Institutionalizing Cultural Knowledge.** Making learning about socioeconomic and cultural groups and their experiences and perspectives an integral part of the school's professional development

Source: Adapted from Raymond D. Terrell and Randall B. Lindsey (2009), *Culturally Proficient Leadership: The Personal Journey Begins Within.* Thousand Oaks, CA: Corwin.

CULTURAL PROFICIENCY IN PRACTICE

Culturally proficient educational practices are embedded in schools and organizations throughout the United States and Canada. The tools of cultural proficiency guide educators to address issues that arise out of diversity. An increasing number of leaders are making strong commitments to culturally proficient leadership, instruction, and community engagement through being responsible for their own learning and development:

- The Wichita, Kansas, School District 259 has established an Office of Cultural Proficiency and is engaging all district employees in related professional development.
- The Howard County Public Schools in Maryland has established the position of Coordinator of Cultural Proficiency to guide professional development throughout county schools.
- The Ottawa-Carleton District School Board in Ontario, Canada, is engaged in training leadership teams and instructional coaches in use of the tools of cultural proficiency.

- The York Region District School Board in Ontario, Canada, is embedding the tools of cultural proficiency in its leadership development programs.
- The Medical Center at the University of California, San Diego, has trained all 3,500 managers, staff, and doctors in the approach. It has incorporated the essential elements into its core competencies used for performance appraisal and related the essential elements to the core values of the hospital, which are printed on the ID badges that staff wear every day.
- Numerous schools in the California communities of San Marcos, Sacramento, Temecula, and Poway have embedded cultural proficiency in their shared visions and are using the tools of cultural proficiency to guide their instructional programs.
- The Commonwealth of Massachusetts Commissioner of Education has endorsed cultural proficiency as the approach he thinks will help close the achievement gap in Massachusetts schools.
- The national U.S. offices of the Presbyterian Church (PC) have adopted a Cultural Proficiency Initiative to help transform the cultural environment of the PC from "one of legalistic compliance with secular affirmative action and equal employment opportunity laws to one of genuine caring and valuing of all humanity where relationship building and God's agape love are modeled."[4]

JUST THE BEGINNING

The purpose of this chapter was to summarize what we are learning about social justice and ways cultural proficiency serves socially just ends. For many school leaders, cultural proficiency is just the beginning of a journey toward socially just practices within the larger school communities they serve. These leaders often begin their journeys with the first steps of opening the school gates to become an inclusive member of the community. Opening the gate comes from the awareness of what it takes to do

Social justice moves leaders from awareness to action, *from skill to* will, *from them to* us, *and from when to* now!

the right thing on behalf of the children and youth within that community. Social justice moves leaders from awareness to *action,* from skill to *will,* from them to *us,* and from when to *now!*

NOTES

1. It is important to note that the achievement gap has been known within education circles since 1971 when the initial report from the National Association of Educational Practice (NAEP) quantified and described the achievement gap in terms of race and gender. NAEP has issued updates every 2 years since 1971, but it was not until the late 1990s, with the issuance of the update of ESEA Title I known as *No Child Left Behind,* that discussion of the achievement gap gained currency *within* education circles let alone within the broader communities we serve.

2. The conceptual framework first appeared in Randall B. Lindsey, Kikanza Nuri Robins, & Raymond D. Terrell (2009), *Cultural Proficiency: A Manual for School Leaders* (3rd ed.), Thousand Oaks, CA: Corwin, pp. 59–60.

3. This section article is adapted from Delores B. Lindsey, Raymond D. Terrell, Kikanza J. Nuri, and Randall B. Lindsey (April/May, 2010), "Focus on Assets, Overcome Barriers," *Leadership, 39*(5), 12–15.

4. The Advocacy Committee for Racial Ethnic Concerns (ACREC). (2004). *Task Force to Examine GA Entities: Report on Creating a Climate for Change Within the Presbyterian Church (U.S.A.),* Section VII: Summary (Recommendation to the 216th General Assembly).

REFERENCES

American Recovery and Reinvestment Act of 2009, Public Law 111–5 (2009).

Collins, J., & Porras, J. (1997). *Built to last: Successful habits of visionary companies.* New York: Harper.

Hilliard, A. (1991). Do we have the will to educate all children? *Educational Leadership, 40*(1), 31–36.

Lindsey, D. B., Terrell, R. D., Nuri, K. J., & Lindsey, R. B. (2010, April/May). Focus on assets, overcome barriers. *Leadership, 39*(5), 12–15.

Lindsey, R. B., Nuri Robins, K. J., & Terrell, R. D. (2009). *Cultural proficiency: A manual for school leaders* (3rd ed.). Thousand Oaks, CA: Corwin.

North, C. (2008). What is all this talk about "social justice"? Mapping the terrain of education's latest catchphrase. *Teachers College Record, 110*(6), 1182–1206.

Senge, P. M., Cambron-McCabe, N. H., Lucas, T., Smith, B., Dutton, J., Kleiner, A., et al. (Eds.). (2000). *Schools that learn: A Fifth Discipline fieldbook for educators, parents, and everyone who cares about education.* New York: Doubleday.

Terrell, R. D., & Lindsey, R. B. (2009). *Culturally proficient leadership: The personal journey begins within.* Thousand Oaks, CA: Corwin.

CHAPTER THREE

BECOMING AN EQUITY-ORIENTED CHANGE AGENT

LINDA SKRLA, KATHRYN BELL MCKENZIE, AND JAMES JOSEPH SCHEURICH

Change does not roll in on the wheels of inevitability, but comes through continuous struggle.

—Martin Luther King, Jr.

Equity audits are tools that you can use to improve equity within your school or district. They will reveal patterns of equity and inequity in three broad areas of the system in place in your schools and districts. However, just knowing that the inequities and equities exist will not automatically lead to a plan for change. In this chapter, we specifically focus on the leader who will be using the equity audit. In other words, our focus here is on you.

What kind of understanding do you need to have to be able to use these tools with your colleagues? It is not as if all of your

Source: From Skrla, L., McKenzie, K. B., and Scheurich, J. J. (2009). *Using Equity Audits to Create Equitable and Excellent Schools,* Chapter 8. Thousand Oaks, CA: Corwin. Reprinted with permission.

fellow teachers, administrators, professional staff, and so forth are just going to immediately and totally embrace equity tools or even equity itself. Indeed, we can virtually promise that you are going to run into multiple kinds and different degrees of resistance.

Some colleagues will just not want to change what they have always done or what they have always thought. Other colleagues will hold conscious or unconscious prejudices against children of color, children whose parents have low incomes, children with learning differences, children whose home languages and cultures are different than the mainstream, and so on. Still other colleagues will just not like you or the way you approach change. Thus, it becomes critically important to figure out how to work as a leader with your colleagues in a way that will facilitate change over time.

Being a change agent, an equity agent, or a civil rights worker, as we called this kind of work in our first Corwin book *Leadership for Equity and Excellence* (Scheurich & Skrla, 2003), is not easy. In fact, it is very hard work. What we will do in this chapter, drawing on our own range of experiences as change agents or civil rights workers in schools, districts, and universities, is provide some advice that we hope will help you.

CHARACTERISTICS OF AN
EQUITY-ORIENTED CHANGE AGENT (EOCA)

EOCA Has an Equity Attitude

We imagine that you have heard the argument that the "means to an end" or a goal must have the same basic qualities as the "end" you have in mind. In other words, if a school leader wants teachers to be caring and respectful to African American students, that school leader needs to be caring and respectful to teachers. Or if a school leader wants teachers to use more discussion and less direct teaching in the classroom, it would be helpful if the leader used more discussion and less direct talk in teacher meetings. Some would call this

If you want your colleagues to have an equity attitude toward their students, you need to have an equity attitude toward your colleagues. . . . If you do not treat all adults this way, your means undermine your ends.

modeling (e.g., Bandura & Walters, 1963). You model what you want others to learn and do. Thus, if you want your colleagues to have an equity attitude toward their students, you need to have an equity attitude toward your colleagues.

What does it mean, though, to have an equity attitude toward your colleagues? To us, it means that no matter what your colleagues' personalities are, no matter what their attitudes or assumptions are, no matter what their prejudices and biases are (we will discuss later "courageous" conversations [Singleton & Linton, 2006]), you treat them with respect, appreciation, and care. If in an equity-oriented school, we want to foster all adults treating all children with respect, appreciation, and care, then we must treat all adults the very same way. If we do not do this, we undermine where we are trying to go—creating an equity-oriented school that serves all children well. Thus, if you do not treat all adults this way, your *means* undermine your *ends*.

Of course, this is easy to say and very hard to do. We all have colleagues who are negative or cynical or who do not seem to care or who just seem to be interested in her or his paycheck or who have hostility or other negative judgments about the school's children or parents or neighborhoods. We all have colleagues we do not think should even be working in our schools. We have colleagues who have short tempers. We have colleagues who will not cooperate or will not carry their fair share of the work. We have colleagues whom we do not trust to be honest with us. We have colleagues who do not think women can be as good leaders as men or who do not think women know as much as men. We have colleagues who are prejudiced toward their colleagues who are of a different race or ethnicity than they are. We have colleagues we think are emotionally troubled. We have colleagues we believe to be destructive. We have colleagues who are always just trying to feather their nests or serve only themselves. We have colleagues who are caught up in the political games or caught up in pleasing those in authority. For many reasons, we will all have colleagues whom we do not want to work with or who are hard to work with.

However, we are strongly recommending that to have an equity attitude and to create a school or district that succeeds equitably with all children, it is necessary to treat *everyone* with respect, appreciation, and care—no exceptions. This does not mean, though, that problems do not get addressed. This does not mean that prejudice, bias, destructiveness, insensitivity, and so forth do not get addressed. In fact, we would argue that addressing difficult issues and having courageous conversations (defined further below) are necessary aspects of treating everyone with respect, appreciation, and care. In fact, we would argue the lack of courageous conversations is disrespectful to others. But addressing difficult issues and having courageous conversations must always be done in interactions that are characterized by respect, appreciation, and care toward everyone.

EOCA Avoids Demonizations

This characteristic is closely connected to the prior one. Demonizations are characterizing someone wholly by one negative characteristic or characterizing someone as totally negative. For example, you have repeatedly seen a colleague treating other colleagues in a negative or hostile way, so you characterize that person solely by these actions. Certainly, if the person is consistently negative or hostile, that person may well be as destructive to others, but a demonization is when you see that person as totally characterized by these actions and do not see other characteristics of the person. In other words, people are very complex; they have many characteristics, usually a combination of some positive and some negative. But when you reduce all of who they are to one negative characteristic and then make that characteristic the essence of who they are or all of who they are, that is demonization.

This is especially a problem when you get angry with someone or when someone does something you find hurtful or insensitive. It then becomes worse when someone repeatedly behaves in this same negative way. Eventually, what often happens is that you begin to see this person in terms of one globalized or totalized way—a racist, a sexist, a cynic, dysfunctional, disturbed, and so on.

While it is very seductive and very emotionally satisfying to be able to characterize someone you do not like as wholly a destructive or hurtful person, these judgments or characterizations, these demonizations, are destructive to creating an equity-oriented environment in your school or district. To create an environment that is characterized by the treatment of all children with respect, appreciation, and care, we have to model the treatment of all adults in the very same way.

This "no demonizations" approach, though, does not mean we do not have to have difficult, courageous conversations with our colleagues about the negative ways they are treating students or the negative way they are treating some of their colleagues or the negative ways you perceive they are treating you. It is absolutely necessary to have such conversations even though they are often very difficult, but such difficult conversations will become all but impossible if you are demonizing the person you need to dialogue with.

EOCA Initiates Courageous Conversations

In their book *Courageous Conversations About Race: A Field Guide for Achieving Equity in Schools,* Singleton and Linton (2006) define a "courageous conversation" as one that has the following characteristics:

1. *Engages* those who won't talk

2. *Sustains* the conversation when it gets uncomfortable or diverted

3. *Deepens* the conversation to the point where authentic understanding and meaningful actions occur (p. 16)

In addition, they contend that for educators to engage in courageous conversations, they must commit to four agreements:

1. Stay engaged.

2. Speak your truth.

3. Experience discomfort.

4. Expect and accept nonclosure. (p. 17)

This advice is a good starting point to what we mean by "initiates courageous conversations."

Although Singleton and Linton (2006) are helping educators to have courageous conversations about race, wonderful work on their part and work we all badly need, our focus here is broader than this. We agree that conscious or unconscious, intended or unintended, racism is one of the largest barriers to equitable schools in this country, and we agree that this is one area in which we badly need courageous conversations. Nonetheless, we want to use this concept of courageous conversations to apply to all kinds of difficult conversations we need to have with our colleagues.

Building off of and expanding Singleton and Linton's (2006) definition of a courageous conversation, we want to provide our advice for those wanting to have courageous conversations in their schools:

1. Throughout the conversation, treat everyone with respect, appreciation, and care.

2. Engage with the other person or persons in the fullness of who they are, not just in terms of their problems or the problems you perceive.

3. Stay fairly and openly engaged with everyone in the conversation.

4. Forgive yourself if you fail, become imbalanced, or lose your temper; as soon as you can, return to a fair and open engagement.

5. Be willing to apologize when you make mistakes or treat someone badly.

6. Know that you too have problems and weaknesses and make mistakes and then be willing for those to be part of the conversation; be willing to have others have courageous conversations with you.

7. Do not be afraid to speak your perspective (your truth) while understanding that it is only yours and not necessarily *the Truth.*

8. Be willing to experience discomfort and be willing to experience others as discomforted; do not become afraid or uncomfortable with discomfort and thus rush to remove it.

9. Work to include everyone in the conversation to equitably participate in the conversation.

10. Do not fear anger, resentment, fear itself, or distancing; just keep working to have an engaged conversation.

11. Constantly work to move the conversation to deeper, more open levels.

12. Expect and accept that one or many such conversations will not immediately lead to happy endings or even closure.

None of these is easy to do, and they will require a great deal of practice and experience to get better at them. We too are always working on using these and failing and working on them again and again.

Be willing to experience discomfort and be willing to experience others as discomforted; do not become afraid or uncomfortable with discomfort and thus rush to remove it.

In terms of these conversations, the easiest thing in the world is to believe that we have the Truth and that our judgments of others are almost always correct. However, when we fall for this and become seduced by this kind of egotism, we are undermining an equity consciousness, and we are undermining the creation of an environment characterized by equity toward all, which is what is necessary to create equitable educational environments for all children. In other words, one of our largest barriers to having courageous conversations will not be other people; it will be our own egotisms and ourselves.

Clearly, these kinds of conversations are very difficult. There is little wonder that we all tend to avoid them. They are hard work. They require that we remain as balanced and centered as possible in the midst of difficult emotional pressures. They require that we take risks with our own vulnerabilities, fears, and insecurities. They require the danger of being open with others, even others we do not like. They require courage, not just effort, which is why Singleton and Linton (2006) rightly called them "courageous conversations."

EOCA Demonstrates Persistence

To be an equity-oriented change agent, you must be persistent. The inequities in our environments did not arise yesterday. They are not simple, superficial features of our environments. Typically, they are a deep part of the status quo; people are used to them and depend on them; they are often deeply embedded in daily institutional life. In addition, there are many behavior patterns, institutional rules and procedures, habits, and assumptions of mind that, though they are not in and of themselves inequities, support inequities.

For example, "zero tolerance" is to some degree an effort to make educational environments safe for all children and adults (Epp & Watkinson, 1997). Thus, to enact zero-tolerance policies, rules and procedures get set up. However, one inequitable result that is occurring all across the country is that these zero-tolerance policies are being disproportionately applied to African American boys (Skiba & Noam, 2001). As a result, if equity is our goal, we have to question the policy itself, the rules and procedures designed to implement the policy, and the attitudes and assumptions of those applying those rules and procedures. Some of the aspects of this problem may not be inequitable in and of themselves, but the result or effect may be inequitable.

Thus, to remove embedded inequities of this or any sort requires persistence. For example, changing zero-tolerance policies will not be easy. It will not simply be a matter of questioning such policies once or twice, and then everyone will agree to change them. Unless there has been some catastrophic failure of the policy, changing the policy will require persistence. Indeed, for almost any inequity, removing or changing it will require persistent, long-term effort. It will require constant focus, repeated effort, and endurance.

We know from our own experiences that this kind of persistence is difficult. However, as we said at the beginning of this section, inequities are often deeply embedded in ourselves and our institutional environments. Also, getting change of any sort in both people and institutions is hard work that takes time. Persistence, then, is a key characteristic of an equity-oriented change agent.

EOCA Remains Committed but Patient

Standing right next to persistence is patience. Unfortunately, institutions, policies, practices, and people do not change over time or within one week or one month. If you are persistent but impatient, this will be communicated to those around you with the result being more difficulty and more resistance. If people feel you are impatient with them, they will experience this as a negative judgment. In addition, if you are impatient, you will wear yourself out, and being an equity agent is long-term work, so maintaining over the long term is necessary.

However, when we counsel patience, we are not saying to let changes go too slowly. You can become so patient that you are pushing change at a slow pace. In fact, the tipping point between not patient enough and too patient is a tough one to know. If you try to go too fast, you will undermine all that you are doing; if you try to go too slow, you will undermine all that you are doing. And unfortunately, no yellow flag will suddenly appear to tell you which side of the tipping point you are on.

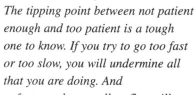

The tipping point between not patient enough and too patient is a tough one to know. If you try to go too fast or too slow, you will undermine all that you are doing. And unfortunately, no yellow flag will suddenly appear to tell you which side of the tipping point you are on.

Judging this point is just flat out hard. Some of your best friends and allies will tell you that you are impatient and trying to move too fast. At the same time, some of your best friends and allies will tell you that you are being too patient and not moving fast enough. Any change agent is always caught between these two, and the line is messy and ambiguous.

The only remedy to this dilemma that we know is to pay attention. If you are trying to push change too fast, many people will resist or complain or say something to you about this. If you are trying to change too slowly, few to none will resist or complain except for those who want the same change you want. The fact is that sometimes you will go too fast, and sometimes you will go too slowly. Just pay attention and try to learn from your experience; this is maybe not the best advice, but it is the best advice we have.

One of the hardest parts of doing equity work is maintaining commitment and patience. You know inequity hurts your students. You know inequity hurts all of us. Yet you cannot successfully facilitate the creation of more equitable environments without patience toward others and patience toward yourself. To be successful, you have to be in this for the long haul, and the long haul requires patience.

EOCA Maintains an Assets Attitude

One of the first people to model for us what we mean by an assets attitude was Dr. Miguel Guajardo, who works with the Llano Grande Center for Research and Development, a community activist center in the Rio Grande Valley of Texas. One of Llano Grande's fundamental assumptions is that in doing community organizing, you start with a focus on the community's assets. Another source of our learning on this has been the work of Dr. Luis Moll and his colleagues (Moll, Amanti, & Gonzalez, 2005; Moll, Amanti, Neff, & Gonzalez, 1992). Moll and his colleagues focus on what they call "the funds of knowledge" that Latino/a students bring with them to school from their families, neighborhoods, and culture. In both of these cases, there is a primary focus on assets rather than on deficits.

We have taken this focus and reframed it as a characteristic of equity workers. If you are going to work on changing a classroom, a school, or a district, it is best to start with the assets that are already in place. And every place and every person has assets, which can be identified. Once you know what these are, you need to constantly build on them as your foundations or starting points for change.

Every place and every person has assets, which can be identified. Once you know what these are, you need to constantly build on them as your foundations or starting points for change.

For example, let's say that the academic performance of your school is inadequate. However, the school has a history of strong support from the community. To use an assets orientation, you would ask how you could build from this history of community support to improve the academic performance of the students. You might bring the community in and involve them in developing ways to improve academic performance. You might develop student–parent contracts on student homework. You might recruit parents to run a Saturday academic academy. There are easily hundreds of different ideas, but the main point is to start with your assets and build them up.

This same approach can be used in working with individuals. Every individual has assets of one sort or another. Since we all want to be valued, validating a person's assets is critically important to building a positive relationship with a person. We are not talking manipulation here; we are talking values. We believe that an equity orientation requires a valuing of all people, no matter who they are. This does not mean that you should not have courageous conversations with someone over difficulties or, say, the mistreatment of children. You do have to have those conversations, but our point is that one key aspect of any conversation and any positive relationship is the recognition and valuing of the person's assets. Then, if you can start with valuing a person's assets, you will have a good foundation to move forward with change or with courageous conversations.

You also need to value your own assets. If you are like us, you are always getting down on yourself for your mistakes. As equity work requires long-term endurance, you have to maintain some reserve of valuing your own assets. We are not talking, though, of feeding our egos. Instead, we are talking about a balanced, persistent awareness that we, too, have assets that need to be valued.

EOCA Maintains a Coherent Focus

To move people or an organization toward more equity requires maintaining a coherent focus. Sonny Donaldson, former superintendent of the Aldine, Texas, school district (a district that has made great progress in closing achievement gaps and raising student performance for all its students) always said to us when we were doing research in his district that "the main thing is to keep the main thing the main thing." While we know this particular saying has been used and said by many others, Sonny Donaldson meant persistently maintaining a coherent focus on improving instruction in his district over time.

This consistent and persistent focus through time is critical to improving equity in your school or district. Indeed, as we have said, creating any kind of sustainable change is very difficult. Change that moves your school or district toward greater equity is truly long, hard work. Thus, to be successful, you will need to maintain your focus over time. In other words, you cannot keep switching areas of focus each week or month. Instead, you need to keep reminding yourself what your focus is and keep communicating that focus. For example, many of the most successful leaders say they say the same thing over and over as they successfully facilitate change in an organization.

CONCLUSION

We fully recognize that understanding and using the seven characteristics of an equity-oriented change agent that we have discussed will be very difficult. We know from our own weekly efforts to maintain these characteristics that we often fail. We sometimes want to demonize someone. We, too, want to avoid courageous conversations. We forget to emphasize an assets orientation. You cannot fail any more frequently than we do.

Thus, a mistake we can all make is to torture ourselves over these failures. Certainly, it is important to recognize our failures and learn from them, and it is not helpful to assume or think we do not all fail constantly in our efforts to lead with an equity attitude. On the other hand, it is an unproductive energy drain to constantly torture ourselves over these failures.

This is yet another place in which finding balance is important. We need to recognize our mistakes, reflect upon them so that we learn, and then move on. This equity work is difficult, but it is also a call to our hearts and minds, a call to make a substantial difference in the lives of *all* of our children. It is, as we have previously said, the civil rights work of our day, and we hope this discussion of the characteristics needed to be an equity-oriented change agent will help you accomplish that work.

REFERENCES

Bandura, A., & Walters, R. H. (1963). *Social learning and personality development.* New York: Holt, Rinehart and Winston.

Epp, J. R., & Watkinson, A. M. (1997). *Systemic violence in education: Promise broken.* Albany: State University of New York Press.

Moll, L. C., Amanti, C., & Gonzalez, N. (2005). *Funds of knowledge: Theorizing practices in households and classrooms.* Mahwah, NJ: Lawrence Erlbaum.

Moll, L. C., Amanti, C., Neff, D., & Gonzalez, N. (1992). Funds of knowledge for teaching: Using a qualitative approach to connect homes and classrooms. *Theory Into Practice, 31*(2), 132–141.

Scheurich, J. J., & Skrla, L. (2003). *Leadership for equity and excellence. Thousand Oaks, CA: Corwin.*

Singleton, G. E., & Linton, C. (2006). *Courageous conversations about race: A field guide for achieving equity in schools.* Thousand Oaks, CA: Corwin.

Skiba, R., & Noam, G. (Eds.). (2001). *Zero tolerance: Can suspension and expulsion keep schools safe? New directions for youth development.* San Francisco: Jossey-Bass.

CHAPTER FOUR

ARE WOMEN PREPARED TO BE SCHOOL SUPERINTENDENTS?

An Essay on the Myths and Misunderstandings

C. CRYSS BRUNNER AND YONG-LYUN KIM

Some social justice scholars suggest that if discrimination against women and people of color was eliminated, their hiring would be one solution for the reported superintendent shortage, smaller applicant pools, and declining quality in candidate pools (Björk & Keyed, 2003; Glass & Björk, 2003; Kowalski, 2003; Tallerico, 2003). The fact that only 18 to 20% of superintendents are women (Brunner & Grogan, 2007) while the

Source: From Brunner, C. C. & Kim, Y. (2010, August). Are women prepared to be school superintendents? An essay on the myths and misunderstandings. *The Journal of Research on Leadership Education*. Reprinted with permission.

candidate pool, from which most educational administrators come, is 75% women (U.S. Census Bureau, 2000) provides some evidence that discrimination exits. Add to this fact the normative expectation that the school superintendent is a man with particular formal education and experiential preparation (experiences not as often enjoyed by, available to, or sought by women), and one is logically left with the assumption that men are the candidates of choice. Could it be that such an assumption includes myths and misunderstandings of *women's* overall preparedness for the role?

THE NATURE OF PREPAREDNESS

The preparedness of educational leaders has been a focus of attention over the past several years (Lankford & Wyckoff, 2003; Levine, 2005). Questions abound related to what constitutes preparation (Baker, Orr, & Young, 2007), what comprises quality preparation, and how preparation should be delivered (Hess & Kelley, 2005; Levine, 2005). For the purposes of this essay, we cast preparedness into three categories: formal, experiential, and personal. *Formal* preparedness is defined by the advanced educational administration training/education that can be received through the conventional coursework and programs offered by all types of institutions (colleges and universities) of higher education. *Experiential* preparedness is characterized by candidates' actual employment record (direct career experiences) and other experiences that could contribute to the quality of professional performance (These include indirect career experiences such as professional relationships—e.g., mentoring.). *Personal* preparedness is defined as one's personal attitude toward the pursuit of or role of the superintendency.

We acknowledge that our categories of preparedness are limited in scope—the topic of preparation is extremely complex. To begin with, when considering formal preparedness, one is struck by the tremendous variety across preparation programs—variety in terms of (to name a few) the (a) type of institution that delivers the program, (b) nature of the curriculum designed, (c) criteria by which applicants are evaluated and selected, (d) amount of coursework required, (e) nature of the delivery system employed (online, face-to-face, hybrid; cohort or individual), (f) cost of the program offered, and (g) background and vitae of faculty who deliver the program. (Most of these elements are discussed in Baker et al., 2007.) Next, when considering experiential preparedness, again, variety dominates the picture. For example, career paths leading to administrative roles vary tremendously. Further, experiences are impacted by gender and race (Brunner & Grogan, 2007). Finally, personal preparedness, while a few trends exist (Young & McLeod, 2001), differs by individual. However, even with these limitations, we believe that recent findings help illuminate and discredit the commonly held answers to the question, "Where are all the women superintendents?" (Glass, 2000).

ARE WOMEN CAPABLE LEADERS?

Misunderstandings of women candidates' capacity and capability exist even when some literature advances information about the effectiveness of women's ways of leading (Alston, 1999; Brunner, 2000; Fulk & DeSanctis, 1999; Grogan, 2000; Mandell & Pherwani, 2003; Mendez-Morse, 2004; Ortiz & Marshall, 1988; Skrla, Reyes, & Scheurich, 2000; Zaccaro, 2001), including their focus on instructional leadership (Faith, 1984; Glass et al. 2000a; Pitner, 1981; Shakeshaft, 1989, 1999). For example, this literature explains that there are gender differences in leadership styles, and attention is drawn to the notion that "women tend to adopt a more democratic or participative style, and men tend to adopt a more autocratic or directive style" (Eagly & Johnson, 1990, cited in Gibson, 1995, p. 258). Several researchers suggested that women should fill higher administrative positions because women's leadership styles often better support current democratic/ participative organizational reform/development (Fresher & Fresher, 1979; Gross & Trask, 1976; Mandel & Pherwani, 2003) and, in particular, the teacher empowerment required for organizational learning (Marks & Seashore-Louis, 1999).

Other studies on leadership style show that women leaders are rated as displaying transformational leadership behaviors more frequently than men leaders (Bycio, Hackett, & Allen, 1995; Yammarino et al., 1997). Women's transformational skills often include a preference for collaboration. Indeed, women leaders on average obtain higher scores on collaborative scales compared to men (Rosenthal, 1998).

AN INFORMED ESSAY: THE APPROACH

In this essay, as we focus on women's preparedness to be school superintendents, we use three categories—(1) formal, (2) experiential, and (3) personal—in order to *respond to* multifaceted insights "on the lack of better representation of women in the superintendency" posed by Thomas Glass (2000) in an article titled, "Where are all the women superintendents?" (p. 28). To empirically inform our work, our responses are primarily grounded in a secondary analysis of the data from the most recent study (of women superintendents and central office administrators) conducted by Brunner and Grogan (2007). In addition, for some comparisons, we conducted a secondary analysis of the data from one of the recent, large, national studies of the superintendency (Glass et al., 2000a). But, before moving to a description of the studies from which the data is taken, we briefly describe Glass's (2000) article and the part it plays in the essay.

Women's transformational skills often include a preference for collaboration. Indeed, women leaders on average obtain higher scores on collaborative scales compared to men (Rosenthal, 1998).

Thomas Glass has been conducting research on the school superintendency over many years and has made significant contributions to the field of educational administration. One of Glass's most important contributions has been his read on the three more recent national studies of the superintendency (Glass, 1992; Glass et al., 2000a; Glass & Franceschini, 2007), studies funded and published by the American Association of School Administrators (AASA)—an association primarily established for school superintendents. Of these studies over decades, only the most recent ones have disaggregated the data by gender.

After the 2000 study, Glass wrote a short article titled, as noted earlier, "Where are all the women superintendents?"—a piece published in the AASA journal *The School Administrator* (2000). In the article, Glass was clear that his asserted "insights" (his term) were his opinions based on his study and experiences of the superintendency over time rather than on any specific factual data. Upon reading the piece, we noted that Glass's insights were a slice of "common understandings" that were often heard from groups and individuals who were speculating on the dearth of women in the superintendency. We also noted, after a secondary analysis of the data from Brunner and Grogan's 2007 study of women superintendents and central office administrators, that many of these common understandings could now be referred to as *myths and misunderstandings,* and that the time had come to either confirm them, further explicate them, or expose their fallacies. The purpose of this essay is to examine Glass's assertions about the dearth of women in the superintendency through the lenses of new data and analysis.

Data Sources: Two National Studies[1]

The AASA National Study of Women Superintendents and Central Office Administrators

The American Association of School Administrators conducted and completed the first nationwide study focused *only* on women in the superintendency and central office positions. This study aimed at providing the most up-to-date, comprehensive information on women and the superintendency (Brunner & Grogan, 2007). This new data informs, extends, and even debunks previous assertions. In particular, because this national study of women superintendents and central office administrators asked the central office administrators the question (Q 105), "If you are not currently a superintendent, do you aspire to the superintendency?" the data could be disaggregated into two categories—those who *did* aspire and those who *did not* aspire to the superintendency. In other words, we now know much more about the women who are poised to move into the superintendency and, for the purposes of this essay, have been able draw on information never before available (see Brunner & Grogan, 2007).

The AASA membership database and data from Market Data Retrieval, the leading U.S. provider of education mailing lists and databases, identified 2,500 women superintendents among 13,728 school districts in 2000, and surveys were mailed. The Brunner and Grogan (2007) study reported that women lead approximately 18% of districts. This increase is about 4% higher than the figure reflected in the 2000 study.

> In addition, 3,000 surveys were sent to women holding central office positions that included the word "superintendent" in the title—Assistant Superintendent or higher. 723 superintendents and 543 central office personnel responded. Nearly 30 percent of the total population of women superintendents is represented in this national sample. (Brunner & Grogan, 2007, p. 155)

The AASA Study of the Superintendency

AASA has conducted consecutive national 10-year studies since1960. The 2000 study included information on the superintendency such as demographic characteristics, school board relationships, superintendents' opinions on specific problems and issues, women and minority participation in the superintendency, as well as professional preparation and superintendents' career patterns. The 2000 study consisted of 90 short-response items and the sample, the largest of any of the Ten-Year Studies, contains responses from 2,262 superintendents across the nation—1,938 men and 294 women (Glass et al., 2000a).

RECONSIDERING MYTHS AND MISUNDERSTANDINGS: THREE FACETS OF PREPAREDNESS

In this large section, we analyze each of Glass's insights about the dearth of women in the superintendency using the lens of three-faceted preparedness: (1) the *formal* or advanced education received through institutions of higher education, (2) the *experiential* or direct career and other professional experiences, and (3) the *personal* or one's attitude toward the pursuit of the superintendency.

Category One: Formal Preparedness

In the first insight, Glass (2000) focused on women's levels of education and degrees—in other words, on women's formal leadership preparedness. As he stated,

Women are not gaining superintendent's credentials in preparation programs. . . . Women also are achieving the doctorate at comparable rates to male candidates. However, about only 10 percent of women in doctoral programs are opting to earn the superintendency credential along with their educational specialist or doctoral degree. (p. 28)

We find Glass's statement difficult to unpack because of the lack of information. To begin with, we do not know where Glass got his information. In order to assert that "only 10 percent of women in doctoral programs are opting to earn the superintendency credential along with their educational specialist or doctoral degree" (Glass, 2000, p. 28), Glass needed to survey a large sample of women in educational specialist or doctoral degree programs, survey a large sample of certification programs, or cite other researchers who conducted such surveys. Since there is no citation in the essay, it is difficult to know where he got his information, though because he uses the number "10 percent," it sounds as if he has factual information.

In contrast, our anecdotal knowledge of superintendency certification programs leaves us with the strong impression that over half of the students pursuing superintendency certification are women. The same is the case with specialist or doctoral degree programs. However, the number of women who are seeking both a doctoral degree *and* superintendency certification remains undocumented. In other words, we can neither support nor refute Glass's statement.

However, we do have additional information that causes us to question Glass's insight. First, over the past two decades, a number of university preparation programs have separated masters and specialist/doctoral degree programs from certification/licensure programs. Thus, in a certain sense, the two must be considered separately. Glass does state that women make up more than 50% of educational administration programs and 50% of doctoral programs. Clearly, women are interested in pursuing educational administration and advancing their educations. Glass does not compare the percentage of women to the percentage of men in doctoral degree programs who opt to earn this credential. Thus, this insight (as he calls it) is, at best, a very weak statement, and at worst, a damaging and misleading piece of information.

The 2007 study also helps address the general topic of women's preparedness for the role of superintendent—an indication of their interest in the role. Larger percentages of women superintendents (57.6% in the 2007 study) than men superintendents (43.4% in the 2000 study) hold doctorate degrees. Related to the superintendency certificate, most women central office administrators (93.5%) who aspire to the superintendency already have a certificate or are currently working toward it (see Table 4.1).

Table 4.1　Highest Degree of Superintendents

Highest Degree	Men Superintendents (2000)	Women Superintendents (2000)	Women Superintendents (2007)	Aspiring Women Administrators (2007)	Non-aspiring Women Administrators (2007)
BA/BS	6 (0.3)	1 (0.3)	1 (0.1)	0 (0)	8 (2.4)
MA in Ed.	155 (7.9)	18 (6.1)	172 (23.8)	48 (23.8)	122 (36.1)
MA not in Ed. (MBA)	9 (0.5)	1 (0.3)	3 (1.2)	0 (0)	5 (1.5)
Specialist	460 (23.6)	31 (10.4)	102 (14.1)	30 (14.9)	51 (15.1)
EDD/ PHD	847 (43.4)	168 (56.6)	416 (57.6)	114 (56.4)	122 (36.1)
Other (MA+)	463 (23.7)	77 (25.9)	28 (3.9)	10 (5.0)	30 (8.9)
Total	1953 (100)	297 (100)	722 (100)	202 (100)	338 (100)

Note: Values in the parentheses are percentages.

According to the U.S. Census Bureau (2000), 60.7% of *all* educational administrators in the United States are women. Based on the 2007 study, among women central office administrators who are not currently positioned in the superintendency, 39.3% aspired to the superintendency (see Table 4.2). These statistics roughly indicate that there are many women who are appropriately and sufficiently qualified in terms of education and certification. Therefore, the matter of the paucity of women in the superintendency may *not* stem from the small pool of credentialed and degreed women applicants.

Table 4.2   Certificates of Women Administrators in 2007 Study

Certificate	Superintendent	Aspiring Women Administrators	Non-aspiring Women Administrators	Total
Yes	650 (90.2)	169 (85.4)	173 (53.2)	992 (79.7)
No	64 (8.9)	13 (6.6)	139 (42.8)	216 (17.4)
Currently working	7 (1.0)	16 (8.1)	13 (4.0)	36 (2.9)
Total	721 (100)	198 (100)	325 (100)	1244 (100)

Note: Values in the parentheses are percentages.

Category Two: Experiential Preparedness

When considering women's experiential preparedness for the superintendency, Glass (2000) stated, "women are not in positions that normally lead to the superintendency" (p. 28). Reconsidering Glass's statement in four discussions below, we (1) problematize the notion of normal; (2) compare the career experiences of men and women; (3) examine women's experience with finance; (4) consider women's mentoring experiences; and finally, (5) discuss the issue of how women's later entrance into administration positions might affect their preparedness.

Assumptions of "Normal"

Using the lens of experiential preparedness, we assert that discussions of career paths (and the benefits of some over others) carry the assumption that particular experiential skills and knowledge result in successful performance in the superintendency. The detailed assumptions of this statement include the notions that (1) there *is* normal experiential knowledge/preparedness that lead(s) to the superintendency; (2) that the "normal" path creates higher-quality superintendents because they have accumulated higher-quality experiential knowledge; and (3) the phrase *normal positions* should be connected to positions filled by men since, when compared historically to other groups, they have moved most easily into the superintendency—an underlying assumption that disregards the possibility that men have moved most easily into the superintendency based in some part on their race and gender rather than solely on their superior experiential preparedness. Because men have overwhelmingly been selected for superintendency positions, their career paths have become the template for success (In this case, "success" means getting the job.). Grounded in these assumptions, Glass asserted that women must do what men do in order to be normal and thus, successful. We note that the term *successful* in Glass's essay is in no way connected to high-quality preparedness or performance. In fact, as of this writing, we know of no study that identifies any measures of quality for superintendency candidates or superintendents. Thus, we disagree with Glass. We believe that this assumed "right way" to pursue the superintendency is less useful and even harmful for women and men who hold new visions of the role—new visions that in part may be the result of unusual experiential preparedness.

We believe that this assumed "right way" to pursue the superintendency is less useful and even harmful for women and men who hold new visions of the role—new visions that in part may be the result of unusual experiential preparedness.

Many scholars who study the school superintendency have noted what the position requires. For example, Kowalski (1999) asserted that the main categories of superintendents' tasks and responsibility can be divided into three domains regardless of the various roles of the superintendency: (1) a wide range of managerial duties, (2) instructional leadership responsibilities, and (3) analytical tasks (e.g., planning and making policy). In traditional or masculine-oriented leadership in the superintendency, the primary role of superintendents focuses more on managerial duties and political strategies than on instruction.

However, considering the social, economic, and educational reforms of schooling, role expectations for the contemporary superintendent could be characterized as one of multifunctional leadership—a role further compounded by new requirements such as instructional leader, collaborator, and culture reconstructionist (Brunner, Grogan, & Björk, 2002; Kowalski, 1999). Given the current focus on academic achievement, alternative routes to the superintendency may be superior to the historical norm. This suggestion gains strength upon an examination of data reflecting what superintendents believe their school boards expect of them. The largest percentage (41.3%), regardless of gender, believes hiring comes if one is a strong educational leader focused on curriculum and instruction (see Table 4.3). If the concept of school reform for enhancing students' achievement was fully reflected in educational administration/superintendency hiring processes, the *normal* career paths leading to the superintendency would include positions focused on curriculum and instruction— positions most often filled by women.

Table 4.3   School Board's Primary Expectations of You as a Superintendent

Role	Men Superintendents (2000)	Women Superintendents (2000)	Women Superintendents (2007)	Total
Education Leader (curriculum and instruction)	742 (38.0)	152 (51.2)	329 (46.3)	1223 (41.3)
Political Leader (board and community relations)	259 (13.3)	26 (8.8)	81 (11.4)	366 (12.4)
Managerial leader (general management, budget & finance)	733 (37.5)	82 (27.6)	173 (24.4)	988 (33.4)
Leader of school reform initiative	52 (2.7)	10 (3.4)	70 (9.9)	132 (4.5)
Community leader (symbolic importance for district and community)	.	.	27 (3.8)	27 (0.9)
Other	154 (7.9)	26 (8.8)	30 (4.2)	210 (7.1)
Total	1953 (100)	297 (100)	710 (100)	2960 (100)

Note: Values in the parentheses are percentages.

Most of the women central office administrators (49%) in the 2007 study were assistant superintendents of curriculum and instruction (see Table 4.4). If experiential preparedness in the area of instructional leadership is important, these women received essential leadership preparation. Thus, we believe that the term *normal* needs a new definition—one that includes experiential preparedness in curriculum and instruction.

Table 4.4   Current Positions of Women Central Office Administrators

Position	Women Administrators (2007)
Deputy Superintendent	86 (8.2)
Chief Academic Officer	10 (2.1)
Assoc/Ass't Superintendent for Human Resource	51 (10.8)
Assoc/Ass't Superintendent for Finance	30 (6.4)
Assoc/Ass't Superintendent for Curriculum and Instruction	231 (48.9)
Assoc/Ass't Superintendent for Operations	9 (1.9)
Assoc/Ass't Superintendent for Administration	30 (6.4)
Assoc/Ass't Superintendent for Support Services	25 (5.3)
Total	472 (100)

Note: Values in the parentheses are percentages.

Comparing Career Paths to the Superintendency

In our secondary analysis of the two large data sets, as Glass implied, we found that when contrasted with men, women's pathways to the superintendency are different. In this discussion, we work within an understanding that the career path of men determines the normal route that most often leads to the superintendency. Thus, this discussion is connected to the experiential preparedness that is acquired with on-the-job experience. Figure 4.1 represents typical pathways that women and men travel to the superintendency. Shakeshaft (1989) first constructed this figure to compare women's and men's pathways to the position, and we further developed it to reflect hierarchy, job opportunity and visibility for career advancement, and job category in terms of line and staff roles.

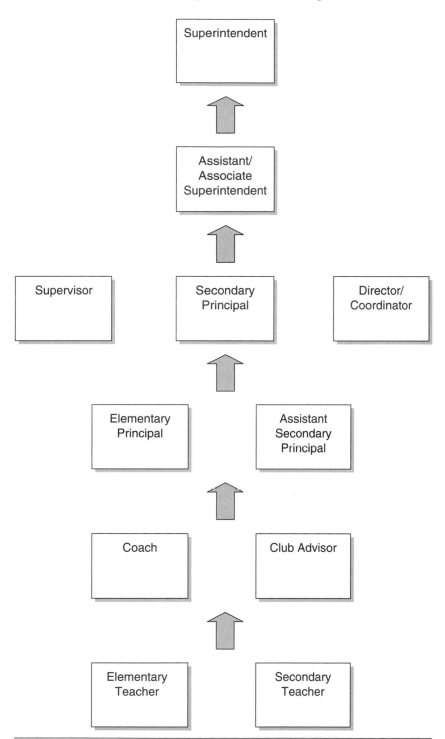

Figure 4.1   Typical Career Paths of Women and Men in Administration

Next, based on analysis of new data (2000 study and 2007 study), we constructed typical career paths of men and women superintendents by assigning numbers/percentages and arrows illustrating position-to-position movement by the majority of the study participants (see Figure 4.2). The typical route for men to the superintendency is secondary teacher (80.2%) → athletic coach (63.0%) → assistant secondary principal (38.0%) → secondary principal (65.0%) → superintendent, while women's typical pathway to the position is elementary (58.2%) or secondary teacher (65.3%) → club advisor (38.0%) → elementary principal (48.3%) → director/coordinator (57.4%) → assistant/associate superintendent (56.0%) → superintendent (Kim & Brunner, 2009) (see Figure 4.2). Note that the survey respondents in this figure were able to check more than one response for the question about their career experiences. For example, if one had teaching experience in both elementary and secondary schools, he or she could respond to both items in the answer. Most women (58.2%) in education started their careers in an elementary teaching position. Although in many cases, secondary school teaching is not the first entry port for women, many of the study's women superintendents had experience teaching in secondary schools (65.3%).

Shakeshaft (1989) argued that women generally do not move into line positions such as the secondary principalship and the superintendency. In our current analysis, however, the typical career paths of women moving toward high levels of administration included both line and staff roles, so the arrows in the women's portion of Figure 4.2 spread to the right and left side as well. Also, Figure 4.2 illustrates that many women started their first administrative positions in elementary schools (48.3%) as principals or in the district office as specialist director/coordinators (57.4%). When in the central office, women are usually in positions related to curriculum and instruction (48.9%, see Table 4.4). Of particular note in Table 4.4—because positions of assistant or associate superintendents do not exist in many small districts—the number and percentage of women in these positions vary according to district size. In contrast to women's typical career paths, arrows in the men's figure were most often placed on the right side, revealing that men's mobility is much more likely to be concentrated in line positions—positions considered to provide greater job opportunities and visibility (see Figure 4.2).

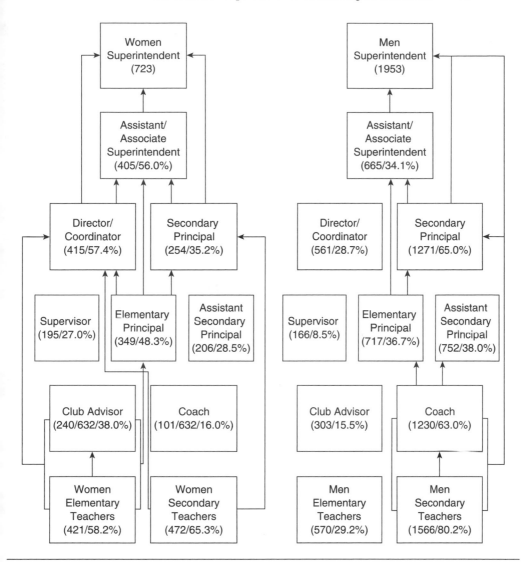

Figure 4.2   A Comparison of Women's and Men's Career Paths

Notes: Arrows are drawn to and from boxes that have a value of 33% or higher. Secondary schools include junior high/middle schools and high schools. This figure is modified from Kim, Y., & Brunner, C. C. (2009). School administrators' career mobility to the superintendency: Gender differences in career development. *Journal of Educational Leadership, 47*(1), 75–107.

As Figure 4.2 shows, women's career pathways are complex and diverse, while men's career pathways are simple and concentrated. This gender difference in career pathways to the superintendency in

When compared to men, women travel in different paths because of the dearth of entry positions into administration.

educational administration could be interpreted in several ways. When compared to men, women travel in different paths because of the dearth of entry positions into administration. For example, women who work in elementary schools often do not have access to positions such as coaching or assistant principalships, since these positions are scarce in elementary schools (Kim & Brunner, 2009). In fact, coaching activities, preferred by men teachers, traditionally have provided junior high and secondary school teachers with an initial step toward administration (Glass, 2000). The lack of coaching and assistant administration positions may lead women to travel along diverse trails of career development rather than through traditional career paths to high levels of administration. While we understand that the visibility of coaches (63% of men superintendents have this experience) may increase aspirants' chances of "being known more broadly" if and when they seek administrative roles, we are not convinced that coaching experience is essential in the preparation of the highest-quality superintendents. However, in the short run, men appear to have an advantage when they move through the very visible entry position of coaching.

Lack of Financial Experience

In one of his insights, Glass (2000) advanced that "women are not as experienced . . . in district-wide fiscal management as men" (p. 28). We question the assumption that women are less prepared than men for fiscal management—both may be underprepared. In order to challenge this assumption, we point out that neither men nor women superintendents, in the 2000 and 2007 studies, indicated that fiscal management was the primary reason they were hired. In the case of women superintendents, they most often thought that their boards had hired them primarily to be educational leaders working with curriculum and instruction (in 2000, 51.2%, and in 2007, 46.3%). While 37.5% of men superintendents (in 2000) thought that boards had hired them to be managerial leader for general management including budget and finance, 38% thought they had been hired to be education leaders (see Table 4.3 on page 69).

While not as great as Glass might have predicted, the percentage differences between men and women superintendents' beliefs about why they were hired are no doubt related to the experiential knowledge and skills that they gained from career pathways (see Kim & Brunner, 2009). To be sure, as Glass suggested, the lack of experience in finance and budget could be a factor that hinders women in their move toward the superintendency. In fact, approximately 77% of women superintendents, compared to approximately 25% of men, believe that school board members *perceive* that women are less qualified than men in the area of finance (see Table 4.10 on page 85). We are not fully persuaded, however, that women's perceptions and lack of experience are as large a barrier as Glass implies. We advance this notion in light of the current increased national attention to academic achievement that we noted above. School board member's perceptions of the ideal superintendent are changing to include curriculum and instruction leadership. Glass admits in his essay, "This situation [the focus on finance] may be changing as many boards are now looking for superintendent leadership in raising test scores and meeting the requirements of state-mandated, high-stakes assessment systems" (p. 30).

We find that while only 6.4% of women central office administrators work as associate or assistant superintendent for finance, 49% of the women central office administrators currently have positions as associate or assistant superintendent for curriculum and instruction and are obviously ready to fill the superintendency as strong educational leaders focused on academic achievement (see Table 4.4 on page 70).

Lack of Mentoring Experiences

On the specific topic of mentoring, Glass (2000) asserted that women seem to have a less-developed mentoring system than men. We know of no study that has come to the same conclusion. Glass continued by stating that "this is important since mentors many times act as go-betweens among superintendent candidates and school boards" (p. 28). This last statement leads us to believe that Glass narrowly defines mentoring. In fact, women may receive less mentoring (than men) aimed at gaining a superintendency position. We define mentoring more broadly to include the learning of the competencies required to be an effective superintendent (see McClellan, Ivory, & Dominguez, 2008).

According to the 2000 and 2007 studies, more women administrators have the experience of mentorships than men superintendents. More than 70% of women superintendents (contrasted with 56.3% of men) in both studies have mentors, and about 60% of women central office administrators have mentors (see Table 4.5). In addition, about 77% of women superintendents in the 2007 study had male mentors. It is certain that women administrators are actively using mentorships (see also Gardiner, Enomoto, & Grogan, 2000; Murtadha-Watts, 2000), but perhaps we should examine whether there is a difference in the quality of these experiences.

Table 4.5 Mentorship Experience

Mentor	Men Superintendents (2000)	Women Superintendents (2000)	Women Superintendents (2007)	Aspiring Women Administrators (2007)	Non-aspiring Women Administrators (2007)
Yes	1099 (56.3)	211 (71.0)	520 (72.0)	106 (61.3)	126 (60.0)
No	837 (42.9)	85 (28.6)	196 (27.1)	64 (37.0)	99 (37.7)
Uncertain	15 (0.8)	1 (0.3)	6 (0.8)	3 (1.7)	9 (3.3)
Total	1951 (100)	294 (100)	722 (100)	173 (100)	270 (100)

Note: Values in the parentheses are percentages.

Women Enter Too Late

In one of Glass's (2000) insights about the dearth of women in the superintendency, he notes that "women enter too late" into administrative positions (p. 28). We have evidence that Glass overstated the importance and extent of this phenomenon. Data from the Brunner and Grogan (2007) study bring more information to this insight (see Table 4.6). While 80.6% of men superintendents entered their first administrative positions before 36 years of age, only 50% of women superintendents and administrators aspiring to the superindendency were in their first administrative roles before the age of 36. However, Kim and Brunner (2009) found in a previous study that while men's average age at first superintendency is 42.7 years, women's average age is 47.3. In other words, while most men enter administration earlier than women, they enter the superintendency only 5 years earlier than women.

Table 4.6   Age at First Administrative Position

Age	Men Superintendents (2000)	Women Superintendents (2000)	Women Superintendents (2007)	Aspiring Women Administrators (2007)	Non-aspiring Women Administrators (2007)
30 or younger	1025 (52.8)	62 (21.1)	119 (17.5)	38 (20.0)	48 (16.0)
31–35	540 (27.8)	77 (26.2)	193 (28.3)	61 (32.1)	77 (25.7)
36–40	237 (12.2)	81 (27.6)	174 (25.6)	42 (22.1)	79 (26.3)
41–45	105 (5.4)	48 (16.3)	120 (17.6)	36 (18.9)	70 (23.3)
46 +	36 (1.9)	26 (8.8)	75 (11.0)	13 (6.8)	26 (8.7)
Total	1953 (100)	294 (100)	681 (100)	190 (100)	300 (100)

Note: Values in the parentheses are percentages.

Table 4.7   Years of Classroom Teaching Experience

Years of Experience	Men Superintendent (2000)	Women Superintendent (2000)	Women Superintendent (2007)	Aspiring Women Administrator (2007)	Non-aspiring Women Administrator (2007)
0–5	789 (40.5)	60 (20.2)	159 (22.0)	54 (26.8)	94 (27.7)
6–10	730 (37.5)	120 (40.4)	267 (37.0)	72 (35.6)	92 (27.1)
11–15	294 (15.1)	70 (23.6)	188 (26.0)	51 (25.2)	94 (27.7)
16–20	90 (4.6)	34 (11.4)	80 (11.1)	21 (10.4)	43 (12.7)
21–25	36 (1.8)	11 (3.7)	22 (3.0)	4 (2.0)	14 (4.1)
26 +	8 (0.4)	2 (0.7)	6 (0.8)	0 (0.0)	2 (0.6)
Total	1947 (100)	297 (100)	722 (100)	202 (100)	339 (100)

Note: Values in the parentheses are percentages.

The 5 additional years (created by longer teaching careers and time taken in administrative roles before moving into the superintendency) of experiential preparation (see Table 4.7) could actually be beneficial to superintendents. Wisdom, it is often thought,

The 5 additional years (created by longer teaching careers and time taken in administrative roles before moving into the superintendency) of experiential preparation could actually be beneficial to superintendents.

comes through years of experience. And at a time when knowledge of teaching and learning is of paramount importance for all administrators, we assert that the 5-year time gap—spent in classrooms and administration of curriculum and instruction—could be of greater experiential preparation benefit than previously thought.

Category Three: Personal Preparedness

Glass (2000) observed that for personal reasons, women are not interested in the superintendency. Specifically, women (1) are not interested in finance, (2) are more accustomed to child-centered teaching in elementary classrooms, (3) fear that too much work time will interfere with their family life, (4) are less willing to move to take superintendencies, and (5) have different purposes for being in education. Women's lack of personal preparedness to aspire to or take superintendencies for these reasons is upheld to some extent by the 2007 study, but overall these reasons should be reconsidered.

Women Not Interested in Finance

Glass (2000) asserted, "women are not . . . as interested in district-wide fiscal management as men" (p. 28). However, we are not convinced that Glass has evidence to support his assertion that women *are not as interested.* We can tangentially support Glass's notion with the fact that only 6.4% of the women central office administrators in the 2007 study were Associate or Assistant Superintendents for Finance (see Table 4.4 on page 70). In our view, however, this fact does not necessarily speak to "interest in finance." As noted in the earlier section on career paths, men and women alike move into positions for multiple and complex reasons. To assert, for example, that men move into finance positions *because* the position represents their strong interest is also problematic.

Almost all superintendency positions hold the expectation that the person in the role has financial capability and capacity. Thus, all men and women who aspire to the role are indicating at least some interest in the financial side of district work. We can say that 40% of the women central office administrators in the 2007 study indicated an interest in becoming superintendents, and further, that of the 60% of the women central office administrators who *did not* aspire to the superintendency, the largest percentage of responses (beyond the fact that they were happy in their current position) indicated that the politics of the role dissuaded them, not the financial responsibilities. And finally, we suggest that all central office work includes budgets of some size—yet another opportunity for experiential preparation relative to finance.

Comfort With Child-Centered Work in Elementary Classrooms

We now turn to the 2007 study and look closely at women central office administrators. As mentioned above, approximately 40% of women central office administrators aspire to the superintendency. Women administrators who do not aspire to the superintendency were asked the question, "Why don't you aspire to the superintendency?" (see Table 4.8). The most frequently selected (36%) response from these women was that they were satisfied with their current positions and had no interest in changing jobs. A total of 27.9% of the women answered that the politics of the job did not appeal to them. They next chose respectively "Too much stress (18.6%)," "Superintendent's salary is not high enough for the weight of the job (13.6%)," and "Job demands of the superintendency would interfere with my family responsibilities (11.3%)." Noting the fact that the women's top four responses were *not* commonly gendered and could easily have been chosen by men, Glass's gendered insight becomes much less compelling (see Table 4.8). For example, Glass's assertion that "women are more accustomed to child-centered teaching in elementary classrooms," is not the case in the 2007 study for many women administrators who have already left the elementary classroom and indicated no interest in returning.

Table 4.8   If you do not aspire to the superintendency, please indicate why not

Reasons	Non-aspiring Women Administrators	
	Checked	Not Checked
Too much stress	87 (18.6)	382 (81.4)
I would have to take a cut in salary	13 (2.8)	456 (97.2)
Superintendent's salary is not high enough for the weight of the job	64 (13.6)	405 (86.4)
Job demands of the superintendency would interfere with my family responsibilities	53 (11.3)	416 (88.7)
I'm happy with my current position and have no interest in changing jobs	169 (36.0)	300 (64.0)
I'm not willing to relocate	46 (9.8)	423 (90.2)
Family members would not be willing to relocate	22 (4.7)	447 (95.3)
I don't have sufficient experience	16 (3.4)	453 (96.6)
I don't have sufficient academic training	16 (3.4)	454 (96.6)
Politics of the job don't appeal to me	131 (27.9)	338 (72.1)
Job opportunities are limited because few school boards would ever hire a woman superintendent	18 (3.8)	451 (96.2)
Other	34 (7.2)	435 (92.8)

Note: Values in the parentheses are percentages.

Another question in the Brunner and Grogan (2007) study clearly demonstrates that Glass's assertion was a weak one. In the study, women central office administrators and superintendents were asked the question, "If you had to do it all over again, which career would you choose?" Most of the women (73.1%) responded that they would remain in the same or higher positions—meaning they would remain in school superintendencies or other central office positions. Only 2.4% of them responded that they would rather be "Classroom teachers," and only 9.2% of women superintendents and central office administrators indicated that they would want to get a job "outside of education" (see Table 4.9). Based on this data, we conclude that women educational administrators generally have strong occupational preferences for educational leadership positions and, thus, are personally prepared to be administrators.

Table 4.9   If you had to do it all over again, would you choose a career as . . .

Careers	Women Superintendents (2007)	Women Administrators (2007)	Total
School superintendent	526 (74.0)	123 (27.5)	649 (56.0)
Other central office position	39 (5.5)	159 (35.6)	198 (17.1)
Classroom teacher	14 (2.0)	14 (3.1)	28 (2.4)
Guidance counselor	4 (0.6)	9 (2.0)	13 (1.1)
College professor	18 (2.5)	17 (3.8)	35 (3.0)
Business manager	1 (0.1)	7 (1.6)	8 (0.7)
State agency employee	1 (0.1)	1 (0.2)	2 (0.2)
Intermediate school district administrator	4 (0.6)	5 (1.1)	9 (0.8)
Principal	25 (3.5)	18 (4.0)	43 (3.7)
Private school administrator	5 (0.7)	4 (0.9)	9 (0.8)
Outside of education	54 (7.6)	53 (11.9)	107 (9.2)
Other	20 (2.8)	37 (8.3)	57 (4.9)
Total	711 (100)	447 (100)	1158 (100)

Note: Values in the parentheses are percentages.

Work Time Diminishes Family Life

Glass asserted that women are not interested in the superintendency because the time demands interfere with family life. In contrast, our data (displayed in Table 4.6 on page 77) show that the answer, "Job demands of the superintendency would interfere with my family responsibilities" drew positive responses from only 11.3% of the study participants. Therefore, while we acknowledge that more women might be superintendents if they could depend on a family-life support system just as men superintendents have traditionally depended on their wives to take care of the family (Brunner, 2000), we also believe that Glass overstated this insight regarding the dearth of women in the superintendency. We have evidence pointing to women's interest in the position even when they have families and children.

Unwillingness to Move

When asked why they did not aspire to the superintendency, only 4.7% of women central office administrators indicated that their families were not willing to relocate. Mobility did not appear to be a large concern among women who *do not aspire* to the superintendency. Glass stated that women do not become superintendents without the support of research. We now have evidence that refutes his opinion that women are unwilling to move.

Women Enter Field for Different Purposes

Glass pointed out that because women have many more career choices than in the past, those who choose teaching really want to *stay* in teaching. We believe that this opinion if turned on men would not play out. Men have always had more career choices than women and many have chosen to be teachers. We doubt that the fact that men chose teaching as a career is any indicator of whether they *do or do not* want to be administrators. We cannot know what people want when we have so little information. We have known numbers of men who have been certified as administrators and never became administrators. In brief, this is a weak reason for the low number of women in the superintendency. In other places in this essay, we have noted that most women in the central office are not interested in returning to teaching.

SUMMARY OF ANALYSIS

Formal Preparedness

We found no evidence that women seek superintendency credentials less often than men. In fact, almost all women central office administrators who aspire to the superintendency have their credentials. Further, more women superintendents than men have their doctoral degrees. Without a doubt, women are formally prepared to become superintendents.

Experiential Preparedness

Related to experiential preparedness, there is no evidence that the "normal" route to the superintendency is the route that creates the highest-quality superintendents. The "normal" route is a gendered one because the career paths of men overwhelmingly constructed it. Finally, given the current concerns about academic achievement, new and different routes to the superintendency may be superior to the historical norm.

Women's career paths include much more curriculum and instruction than the career paths of men, a fact that for women creates a career path that includes both line *and staff* positions. Women's career paths, as a result, are complex and diverse, while men's career paths are simple and concentrated. Thus, women gain much more variety in their experiential preparedness, although their various experiences rarely include the narrowly defined finance position. However, we believe it safe to say that anyone seeking the superintendency has confidence in her or his own capacity in finance. We also note that the majority of men and women superintendents report that financial expertise was *not* the *primary* reason they were hired.

Finally, two other misunderstandings related to experiential preparedness were set aside. First, contrary to common belief, women are more often mentored than men. And second, given the most current data, we now have evidence that women on average enter the superintendency only 5 years later than men—a difference that is much shorter than previously reported. We note that these 5 years were most often spent with curriculum- and instruction-related jobs—jobs that may actually add value to women's experiential preparedness for the superintendency.

Personal Preparedness

Regarding personal preparedness or women's attitude toward the pursuit of the superintendency, we addressed five myths or misunderstandings about the dearth of women in the superintendency. The first relates to women's attitudes toward finances. Glass asserted that women are not interested in finances and as a result are not interested in pursuing the superintendency. We acknowledge that only a few women central office administrators are assistant or associate superintendents of finance. However, we can assume that those who aspire (men *and* women) have some interest or capacity in finance since superintendents are ultimately responsible for the financial health of their districts. And we also assume that all central office administrators have oversight in appropriate budget areas and thus, they are aware of and experienced in financial matters. Finally, as support for our assumptions, we note that when asked why they *did not* aspire to the superintendency, women central office administrators responded only 3.4% of the time that they lacked the necessary experience (see Table 4.10).

The last four of the five myths or misunderstandings are related to each other. We found little evidence to support any of these assertions. As is probably assumed true for men, 97% of women central office administrators indicate *no desire* to return to teaching, 89% believe the job would *not* interfere with family life, and 95% indicate that their families are willing to relocate for job purposes. We also note that men have always had the greatest number of occupation choices, and no one assumes that they *want* to stay in teaching because they chose it initially.

CONCLUSIONS AND IMPLICATIONS

Given our discussion of the data, we conclude that women central office administrators are formally, experientially, and personally prepared to become superintendents. Further, we conclude that the negative perceptions surrounding the dearth of women in the superintendency, those that make the women themselves the cause of the dearth, are gendered myths and misunderstandings created by gender bias. We also assert that gendered norms create barriers for women seeking the superintendency. In fact, the 2000 study asked men and women superintendents what barriers to the role exist for women. Some barriers that women thought of as significant included the school board's prejudices against women administrators, school board members' perception that women are not strong managers, and 38% indicated the school board members' perception that women are unqualified to handle budgeting and finances. These barriers relate directly to negative perceptions of women's lack of preparedness.

Table 4.10 Barriers Limiting Administrative Opportunities for Women

Barriers	Men Superintendents (2000)				Women Superintendents (2007)			
	Important	Somewhat Important	Not a Factor	Don't Know	Important	Somewhat Important	Not a Factor	Don't Know
Schools boards do not actively recruit women	153 (7.9)	566 (29.3)	1000 (51.8)	211 (10.9)	196 (27.5)	335 (46.9)	144 (20.2)	39 (5.5)
Lack of mobility of family members	408 (21.1)	978 (50.6)	258 (13.4)	287 (14.9)	321 (44.9)	311 (43.5)	58 (8.1)	25 (3.5)
Mid-management career "glass ceiling"	53 (2.8)	527 (27.5)	927 (48.4)	407 (21.3)	159 (22.6)	322 (45.8)	157 (22.3)	65 (9.2)
Lack of opportunities to gain key experiences prior to seeking the superintendency	142 (7.4)	582 (30.2)	1059 (55.0)	144 (7.5)	168 (23.5)	281 (39.3)	255 (35.7)	11 (1.5)
Lack of professional networks	74 (3.9)	611 (31.8)	1008 (52.5)	226 (11.8)	158 (22.2)	337 (47.4)	196 (27.6)	20 (2.8)
Perception of school board members that women are not strong managers	129 (6.7)	693 (35.9)	834 (43.3)	272 (14.1)	287 (39.9)	280 (38.9)	114 (15.9)	38 (5.3)
Perception of school board members that women are unqualified to handle budgeting and finances	70 (3.6)	435 (22.5)	1168 (60.5)	257 (13.3)	272 (38.0)	281 (39.2)	125 (17.5)	38 (5.3)

(Continued)

Table 4.10 (Continued)

Barriers	Men Superintendents (2000)				Women Superintendents (2007)			
	Important	Somewhat Important	Not a Factor	Don't Know	Important	Somewhat Important	Not a Factor	Don't Know
Perception that women will allow their emotions to influence administrative decisions	99 (5.1)	553 (28.7)	979 (50.7)	299 (15.5)	218 (30.4)	295 (41.1)	164 (22.9)	40 (5.6)
The nature of superintendents' work makes it an unattractive career choice	252 (13.1)	693 (36.0)	749 (38.9)	233 (12.1)	165 (23.1)	335 (46.9)	198 (27.7)	17 (2.4)
Lack of mentors/mentoring in school districts	116 (6.0)	670 (34.8)	884 (45.9)	255 (13.2)	151 (21.1)	364 (50.8)	185 (25.8)	16 (2.2)
Perception that women are not politically astute	·	·	·	·	148 (20.7)	275 (38.5)	250 (35.0)	42 (5.9)
Perception that instructional and curricular orientations or emphases limit administrative and managerial interests and skills	·	·	·	·	104 (14.5)	305 (42.7)	244 (34.1)	62 (8.7)

Note: Values in the parentheses are percentages.

In sum, we believe that women central office administrators who aspire and women seated in the superintendency meet and even exceed all formal, experiential, and personal preparedness requirements. Further, while some of the preparedness components for women are different from those gained by men, we suggest that the variation in career path and the concentration on curriculum and instruction may render women better and more thoroughly prepared than men. Overall, we find aspiring and seated women superintendents well-prepared for the superintendency and can offer no explanation for the dearth of women in the superintendency other than the fact that long-held biases, while perhaps lessening their hold, are still afoot during superintendency and other administrative selection processes.

Implications for Action: Improving Preparation

In conclusion, we identify three implications for future action. First, preparation programs must engage in course work conversations that lay bare the issue of gender bias. We recognize that gender bias is a societal issue and one perpetuated by both women and men. One way to address this difficult topic includes conducting such conversations in places that allow anonymous participation. Efforts of this type have proven powerful in many cases (see Brunner, Hammel, & Miller, 2003; Brunner, Opsal, & Oliva, 2006).

Students cannot learn new ways of doing the superintendency if they are strictly imitating others who are currently in the role.

Second, with the clear acknowledgment of experiential preparedness, preparation programs must include all manner of technology-based strategies for more creative approaches to simulating parts of the role that are not currently practiced by the typical superintendent. We tend to count on internships to provide experiential training. The limitations of this model are obvious if we actually believe the superintendency must change. Students cannot learn new ways of doing the superintendency if they are strictly imitating others who are currently in the role. In addition, as professors of educational administration most often come from practice, the formal layer of preparation must also be addressed. In particular, the "School Superintendency" class is most often taught by men (from the perspective of their experiences) because they dominate the positions in the field—thus creating another barrier (since women typically have different experiential preparation) for women who aspire to the role. In our view, one of the only ways to address the multi layers of the reenactment and reinforcement of the status quo is through the use of virtual spaces—spaces in which gender and other forms of difference can be set aside during development programs (see Brunner et al., 2003, 2006).

Finally, preparation programs could be reshaped to value complexity and variety in addition to the commonly offered skill development. Clearly, the superintendency in particular is a role that includes a wide variety and complexity of responsibilities. The role is broader than any other in the educational system. A systematic effort could be made to draw attention to how various educational career paths support preparedness for the superintendency. When considering the variety and complexity of superintendent responsibilities, we understand that the primary focus must be on academic achievement for students. We believe that many preparation programs already provide an emphasis in this area, but research is still showing that superintendents do very little related to curriculum and instruction, and certainly have not valued it over other areas of preparation. Thus, while there are efforts in this direction, their impact is not yet evidenced in the field. In brief, we are calling for a reshaped superintendency—one that requires the experiences most often chosen by women aspirants.

NOTE

1. This essay is based on a portion of the data set collected in a large study (Brunner & Grogan, 2007) focused on women superintendents and women central office administrators. Therefore, the brief methods section is similar to portions of other publications written from the same database. Further, in this essay, we use the year 2007 when referring to the Brunner and Grogan data in order to simplify the text. Data was first available in 2005.

REFERENCES

Alston, J. A. (1999). Climbing hills and mountains: Black females making it to the superintendency. In C. C. Brunner (Ed.), *Sacred dreams: Women and the superintendency* (pp. 79–90). Albany: State University of New York Press.

Baker, B. D., Orr, M. T., & Young, M. D. (2007). Academic drift, institutional production, and professional distribution of graduate degrees in educational leadership. *Educational Administration Quarterly, 43*(3), 279–318.

Björk, L. G., & Keyed, J. L. (2003). Guest editors' introduction: Who will lead? Examining the superintendent shortage. *Journal of School Leadership, 13*(3), 256–263.

Brunner, C. C. (2000). *Principles of power: Women in the superintendency.* Albany: State University of New York.

Brunner, C. C., & Grogan, M. (2007). *Women leading school systems: Uncommon roads to fulfillment.* Lanham, MD: Rowman & Littlefield.

Brunner, C. C., Grogan, M., & Björk, L. (2002). Shifts in the discourse defining the superintendency: Historical and current foundations of the position. In J. Murphy (Ed.), *The challenge of school leadership: Redefining leadership for the 21st century—National Society for the Study of Education yearbook* (pp. 211–238). Chicago: University of Chicago Press.

Brunner, C. C., Hammel, K., & Miller, M. D. (2003). Transforming leadership preparation for social justice: Dissatisfaction, inspiration, and rebirth—An exemplar. In F. Lunenburg & C. Carr (Ed.), *Professors and practitioners: Building bridges through leadership: NCPEA yearbook—2003* (pp. 70–84). Toronto, ON, Canada: Scarecrow Education.

Brunner, C. C., Opsal, C., & Oliva, M. (2006). Disrupting identity: Fertile soil for raising social consciousness in educational leaders. In C. Marshall & M. Oliva (Eds.), *Leading for Social Justice: Making revolutions in education* (pp. 214–232). Thousand Oaks, CA: Sage.

Bycio, P., Hackett, R. D., & Allen, J. S. (1995). Further assessments of Bass's (1985) conceptualization of transactional and transformational leadership. *Journal of Applied Psychology, 80,* 468–478.

Faith, G. C. (1984). Women in educational administration: A research profile. *Educational Forum, 49,* 65–79.

Fresher, J. M., & Fresher, R. S. (1979). Educational administration: A feminine profession. *Educational Administration Quarterly, 15*(2), 2–13.

Fulk, J., & DeSanctis, G. (1999). Articulation of communication technology and organizational form. In J. M. Sharfritz & J. S. Ott (2001), *Classics of organization theory* (5th ed., pp. 400–518). Orlando, FL: Harcourt College Publishers.

Gardiner, M. E., Enomoto, E., & Grogan, M. (2000). *Coloring outside the lines: Mentoring women into school leadership.* Albany: State University of New York Press.

Gibson, C.B. (1995). An investigation of gender differences in leadership across four countries. *Journal of International Business Studies, 26*(2), 255–279.

Glass, T. (1992). *The study of the American school superintendency: America's education leaders in a time of reform.* Arlington, VA: American Association of School Administrators.

Glass, T. (2000). Where are all the women superintendents? *School Administrator, 57*(6), 28–32.

Glass, T. & Björk, L. G. (2003). The superintendent shortage: Findings from research on school board residents. *Journal of School Leadership, 13*(3), 265–287.

Glass, T., Björk, L. G., & Brunner, C. C. (2000a). *American Association of School Administrators' ten-year study of the superintendency.* Arlington, VA: American Association of School Administrators.

Glass, T., Björk, L. G., & Brunner, C. C. (2000b). *The study of the American superintendency 2000: A look at the superintendent in the new millennium.* Arlington, VA: American Association of School Administrators, and Lanham, MD: Scarecrow Press.

Glass, T., & Franceschini, L. A. (2007). *The state of the American school superintendency: A mid-decade study.* Lanham, MD: Rowman & Littlefield.

Grogan, M. (2000). Laying the groundwork for a reconception of the superintendency from feminist postmodern perspectives. *Educational Administration Quarterly, 36,* 117–142.

Gross, N., & Trask, A. E. (1976). *The sex factor and the management of schools.* New York: Wiley-Interscience.

Hess, F. M., & Kelly, A. M. (2005, May 18). Learning to lead? *Education Week, 24,* 37.

Kim, Y., & Brunner, C. C. (2007, November). *Career mobility factors and women's access to the superintendency: A structural equation model.* Paper presented at the University Council for Educational Administration National Conference, Arlington, VA.

Kim, Y., & Brunner, C. C. (2009). School administrators' career mobility to the superintendency: Gender differences in career development. *Journal of Educational Leadership, 47*(1), 75–107.

Kowalski, T. (1999). *The school superintendent: Theory, practice, and cases.* Upper Saddle River, NJ: Prentice Hall.

Kowalski, T. (2003). Superintendent shortage: The wrong problem and wrong solutions. *Journal of School Leadership, 13*(3), 288–303.

Lankford, H., & Wyckoff, J. (2003). *The supply of school leaders: A multivariate analysis of administrative certification and transitions to leadership positions.* Albany, NY: University of Albany.

Levine, A. (2005). *Educating school leaders.* New York: The Education Schools Project.

Mandell, B., & Pherwani, S. (2003). Relationship between emotional intelligence and transformational leadership style: A gender comparison. *Journal of Business and Psychology, 17*(3), 387–404.

Marks, H. M., & Seashore-Louis, K. (1999). Teacher empowerment and the capacity for organizational learning. *Educational Administration Quarterly, 35*(5), 707–750.

McClellan, R., Ivory, G., & Dominguez, R. (2008). Distribution of influence, communication, and relational mentoring in the U.S. superintendency. *Mentoring and Tutoring: Partnership in Learning, 16*(3), 346–358.

Méndez-Morse, S. (2004). Constructing mentors: Latina educational leaders' role models and mentors. *Educational Administration Quarterly, 40*(4), 561–590.

Murtadha-Watts, K. (2000). Cleaning up and maintenance in the wake of an urban school administration tempest. *Urban Education, 35*(5) 603–615.

Newton, R. M. (2006). Does recruitment message content normalize the superintendency as male? *Educational Administration Quarterly, 42*(4), 551–577.

Ortiz, F. I., & Marshall, C., (1988). Women in educational administration. In N. Boyan (Ed.), *Handbook of research on educational administration* (pp. 123–141). New York: Longman.

Pitner, N. J. (1981). Hormones and harems: Are the activities of superintending different for a woman? In P. A. Schmuck, W. W. Charters, Jr., & R. O. Carlson (Eds.), *Educational policy and management* (pp. 273–295). New York: Academic Press.

Rosenthal, C. S. (1998). Determinants of collaborative leadership: Civic engagement, gender or organizational norms? *Political Research Quarterly, 51*(4), 847–868.

Shakeshaft, C. (1989). *Women in educational administration.* Newbury Park, CA: Corwin Press.

Shakeshaft, C. (1999). The struggle to create a more gender inclusive profession. In J. Murphy & K. S. Lewis (Eds.), *Handbook of research on educational administration* (2nd ed., pp. 99–118). San Francisco: Jossey-Bass.

Skrla, L., Reyes, P., & Scheurich, J. J. (2000). Sexism, silence, and solutions: Women superintendents speak up and out. *Educational Administration Quarterly, 36*(1), 44–75.

Tallerico, M. (2003). Policy, structural, and school board influences on superintendent supply and demand. *Journal of School Leadership, 13,* 347–364.

U.S. Census Bureau (2000). *Census 2000 equal employment opportunity data.* Retrieved November 10, 2010, from http://www.census .gov/eeo2000/index.html

Yammarino, F. J., Dubinsky, A. J., Comer, L. B., & Johnson, M. A. (1997). Women and transformational and contingent reward leadership: A multiple-levels-of-analysis perspective. *Academy of Management Journal, 40*(1), 205–222.

Young, M. D., & McLeod, S. (2001). Flukes, opportunities, and planned interventions: Factors affecting women's decisions to become school administrators. *Educational Administration Quarterly, 37*(4), 462–502.

Zaccaro, S. J. (2001). *The nature of executive leadership: A conceptual and empirical analysis of success.* Washington, DC: American Psychological Association.

CHAPTER FIVE

LEADING SCHOOLS
OF CHARACTER

MARVIN W. BERKOWITZ

The title of this volume, *Leadership for Social Justice and Democracy in Our Schools,* can have two connotations. The first is that we want school leaders who create schools that are just and democratic, i.e., schools where all stakeholders treat each other fairly and make ethical decisions, and that those decisions are made in a collaborative, democratic fashion. The second is that we want leaders who create schools that promote the development of justice and democratic knowledge, skills, and dispositions in their students. Fortunately, these two interpretations are inextricably intertwined; i.e., creating fair and democratic schools promotes the development of justice and democratic competencies and proclivities in students who attend such schools (Dewey, 1909). When I worked in Lawrence Kohlberg's Just Community Schools (Power, Higgins, & Kohlberg, 1989), in the late 1970s, that is precisely what we were doing. The Just Community Schools model was designed to create democratic schools in which the democratic process was always directed toward decisions that promoted both a sense of community and just processes. While such schools are ambitious and only infrequently established, they point directly to the impact of living in a fair and democratic community on the moral development of the members of that community.

In this chapter, I will take a more focused look at the role of school leadership in both transforming schools into the types of institutions where democratic decision making flourishes and, consequently, where students develop moral and civic character. In doing so, I will not focus exclusively on those outcomes, but rather will take a more global perspective on the aspects of school leaders and leadership that nurture the transformation of schools into what we will call "schools of character." First, I will make certain premises explicit and then will define some key terms.

Creating fair and democratic schools promotes the development of justice and democratic competencies and proclivities in students who attend such schools.

PREMISES

The first premise is that *the best way to make a more just and caring world is to make more just and caring people.* As a developmental psychologist, I generally embrace the anonymous statement that "a child is the only known substance from which a responsible adult can be made." If we want a more moral world, then we need more moral people, and the best way to get more moral people is to invest in the parenting, education, and general socialization of children.

The second premise is that *schools can, should, and inevitably will shape the development of students.* Throughout this chapter, I will be relying upon and therefore introducing the reader to a series of exemplary school leaders in order to concretize the points I will be making. So let me now introduce the first of them. Avis Glaze recently retired as Ontario's (Canada) first Chief Student Achievement Officer and founding CEO of the Literacy and Numeracy Secretariat. She was also charged with designing and implementing character education for the approximately 5,000 schools in the Province of Ontario, which ranged from small Inuit schools near the Arctic Circle to large, widely diverse urban schools in Toronto. Prior to this job, she served as a teacher, counselor, school administrator, and district administrator. Her successes in both academic achievement (including reducing the achievement gap) and character development have led to multiple recognitions for both her and Ontario education. One thing she taught me (among many) is something she frequently tells educators: "We [in the field of education] are in the business of enhancing the life chances of our students, and influencing people, communities, and organizations."

Unlike Avis Glaze, I am not an educator (despite being an endowed professor of education and having taught college students for nearly 40 years). Rather, my training is as a developmental psychologist. I have found this to be invaluable as I work with teachers and administrators. I see schools through the lens of how they impact the development of children. James Comer (1999), a pioneer in developmentally informed school reform, has opined,

> The responsibility of every society is to provide children with adults and with institutions that can help them develop and learn. . . . With such help they will have a reasonable chance to meet their adult tasks. . . . Nonetheless, many in the modern school reform movement are concerned about issues of power . . .; test scores; and what parents, teachers, administrators, politicians want—not what children need to grow, develop, and meet their adult tasks and responsibilities. (p. xx)

If we truly want schools that contribute meaningfully to the socialization of the next generation of ethical, democratic citizens, then we have to look through the lens of child development, as we are, after all, in the business of changing people.

The third premise is that *the changes schools make in students cannot and should not be limited to the intellectual and academic; rather, they will and should encompass the moral and civic development of students.* In acknowledging that schools must focus on intellectual growth, Dewey (1909) argued that "it is not out of the question to aim at making the methods of learning . . . such that they will render behavior more enlightened," by which he means more moral (p. 3). For Dewey, the school has a fundamental moral purpose, and morality entails that which will "take effect in conduct and improve it, make it better than it otherwise would be" (p. 1). Kohlberg and Mayer (1972) explicitly echoed Dewey in their paper entitled "Development as the Aim of Education: The Dewey view." Changing people, specifically students in schools, must and will inevitably entail impacting their moral growth, i.e., the development of their moral and civic character.

The fourth premise is that *for schools to optimally impact the development of student character (both moral and civic), they must be moral and democratic institutions.* Durkheim (1961) argued that (1) society needs schools to foster the moral development of students for the very survival of society, and (2) to do this, schools have to promote both a sense of community and democratic processes. Dewey (1909) has similarly argued that "to an extent characteristic of no other institution, save that of the state itself, the school has the power to modify the social order" (p. v). This dual refrain, that schooling is necessarily a moral endeavor and the moral nature of schools (their culture and climate, their hidden curricula, etc.) directly impacts the moral development of students, is a long-standing and widely accepted one (e.g., Boyer, 1995; Feinberg, 1990; Jackson, Boostrom, & Hansen, 1993; Power et al., 1989; Sizer & Sizer, 1999; Sockett, 1993).

The fifth and final premise is that *for schools to become the kinds of moral and democratic institutions that promote the development of students, they need leaders who understand, prioritize, and have the leadership competencies to nurture such institutional growth.* This will indeed be the focus of the bulk of this chapter. It is critical that school leaders further understand and embrace the fact that student development is a core goal, that school development is necessary for student development to be optimized, and that the personal and professional development of the leader is necessary for both of these to happen. In other words, as Wagner and Kegan (2006) have argued, "transforming organizations . . . requires very different kinds of leaders—ones who recognize that they, as individuals, may have to change in order to lead the necessary organizational changes" (p. 11). This requires courage, insight, and altruism. Brenda Logan, former principal at Hazelwood Elementary School in Louisville, Kentucky, said that she started thinking that all that needed to change was students, "but my big 'aha' was when it hit me that reform means many different types of changes, one of which might be to change or alter my own behavior and the possible impact on the behavior of the staff" (personal communication, 2010). This is a daunting revelation to many educators who dip their toes in the turgid waters of comprehensive school reform.

MAPPING THE TERRAIN

Character education is comprehensive school reform that supports both academic achievement and positive student development. When I use the term *character education,* I am using it broadly to include related terms like positive psychology, prosocial education, and social-emotional learning. In doing so, I will use the following definition: "[C]haracter education . . . is the process of intentionally fostering . . . the composite of those characteristics of the individual that directly motivate and enable him or her to act as a moral agent, that is, to do the right thing" (Berkowitz & Puka, 2009, p. 109). Furthermore, this view of character education is fundamentally based in changing the entire culture, and consequently many of the practices, of a school. It therefore makes sense that the principal in a school is the centerpiece of character education's quality and success.

Character education is comprehensive school reform that supports both academic achievement and positive student development. . . . This view of character education is fundamentally based in changing the entire culture, and consequently many of the practices, of a school.

Before we proceed much further, we need to spend a little time talking about what counts as school leadership. When asked to do presentations or workshops on educational leadership, I have learned to ask what the person or organization inviting me means by leadership in an educational context. I have found the following meanings are the most common ones intended:

- School (or district) administration
- Teacher leadership
- Student leadership

And I have discovered that educators (and others interested in educational leadership) often conflate these leadership variations.

What it takes to get students to develop leadership competencies and values is quite different from what a school principal needs to do in order to effectively act as a leader, for example. In this chapter, I am concerned only with the school administration (although almost all of what I will say also applies to district administration), and in this regard I am mostly concerned with the lead principal of the school.

This chapter will essentially be an examination of the characteristics of principals who can most effectively lead the comprehensive school reform process of shepherding the evolution of a school into a true "school of character": a school that promotes the sustained development of those inclinations and capacities of an effective moral agent, one who regularly "does good" in the world, including the desire and capacity to act as a democratic citizen. It is worth reiterating that such schools also produce higher levels of academic achievement (Benninga, Berkowitz, Kuehn, & Smith, 2003; Berkowitz & Bier, 2005; Payton et al., 2008). Essentially, good character education is good education, and good character education leadership is good school leadership.

THE CONTEXT

My current position is an endowed chair in character education and part of the regional Des Lee Collaborative Vision (DLCV). The DLCV is a broadly interdisciplinary network of endowed professors in the St. Louis region. Each professor has one foot in the academy and one foot in the community, with the obligation to link the two in order to serve disadvantaged youth.

My community partner is CHARACTERplus, a professional development division of the Cooperating School Districts of St. Louis. Within CHARACTERplus, I spend the majority of my time working with the Leadership Academy in Character Education (LACE). LACE is a complex professional development experience, entailing (in part) monthly full-day meetings and monthly written assignments as the core of a yearlong curriculum that systematically builds a site-specific implementation plan.

These assignments are strategic thought experiments and implementation steps designed to move the participant (the school leader) to both deeper understanding and better practice.

Each assignment is read either by me or my assistant and detailed written feedback is provided. The feedback is designed to both affirm and to challenge the participant, in a form of written mentoring. A cycle of collaborative site-based reflection and brainstorming generates the report, to which we respond with detailed written constructive feedback.

It is through this process that I have watched hundreds of school leaders grapple with the meaning of character education, with understanding what a truly great school entails, and with facing their own strengths and weaknesses as school leaders. Furthermore, I have watched many of these principals continue to lead their schools through lengthy and successful reform processes, and of course I have watched others not try and yet others try and not succeed. This, then, is the context in which I will present key issues in leading schools of character.

A Word About Outcomes

As the accountability movement in education has taught us, good education demands a clear understanding of the outcome goals of education before we can ever begin to talk about pedagogy. It is no different in character education. Enthusiastic school leaders often surge forward in designing their character education initiatives without spending the time to consider what those initiatives are intended to promote. Or they have a clear set of outcomes but the methods they adopt are not aligned with those outcomes. For example, one principal approached me quite enthusiastically and announced, "Marvin, I just have to tell you about our new character education initiative!" When I encouraged him, he said he first wanted to tell me what instigated this new initiative. Apparently, they had uncovered a significant amount of cheating in his high school and upon looking at national research (e.g., McCabe, 1999), realized that they had likely had their heads in the sand on this national epidemic. When I lauded him on using this "teachable moment" as a presenting symptom to spur school reform, he proudly announced how they were implementing character education. "Service-learning. It is going to be school-wide and across the curriculum, and we are investing heavily in professional development to support it." So I said to him, "That is wonderful. Service-learning is a great academic and character education method, with solid research to support its impact on academic achievement and various aspects of character development. And investing in your staff and their expertise is great leadership. But I have one question. What on earth does service-learning have to do with academic integrity?" He was stunned. They had never even considered whether the implementation strategy (service-learning) was aligned with (would lead to) their targeted outcome (academic integrity).

Schools need to start at the end, i.e., with the desired outcomes. One way I have addressed this when consulting with schools is to ask the question, "If your school was wildly successful at promoting character education, and if students entered your school at the earliest grade level and stayed until the latest grade level, what would be different about them as a direct result of your character education initiative?" This usually engenders great reflective discussions and more enlightened goals. When such goals are specific and developmentally relevant, then the basis is there for building an initiative, which should include a strong consideration of both (1) developmental processes for the selected outcomes and (2) research-based and aligned effective methods that build upon those developmental principles. In essence this is a "logic model," in other words, an articulation and justification of the logical connections among goals, methods, and assessment.

"GETTING IT": THE PRINCIPAL'S FOUNDATION

As already noted, effective school-based character education starts with the principal. That does not mean someone else cannot be the catalyst for character-focused school reform. Of course, when we look at a school district, then the superintendent is the analogous lead person. For example, Sheldon Berman led the Hudson Public School District (MA) to recognition as, at that time, only the third National District of Character in 2001. For him, the fundamental purpose of schooling was (and is, as he is now the superintendent of the Jefferson County Public Schools, KY) the development of social responsibility, democratic citizenship, and moral character of students (Berman, 1997). He articulated his vision and worked strategically to put the human and other resources in place to focus his district on this goal. He even went so far as to have his new high school architecturally designed to accommodate democratic deliberation among students, service-learning, and his broader mission. Matt Klosterman, current superintendent, and Bill Porzukowiak, former assistant superintendent, of the Belleville (IL) 118 School District, made a strategic decision that building and district leadership was critical to school improvement in general and character education in particular. Over the past decade, they have strategically sent every school and district administrator through LACE. They have been recognized by the State of Illinois for academic achievement, especially reducing the achievement gap, and have twice been named a finalist as a National District of Character.

One exercise I do with principals is to ask them first if they can tell me their mission statements verbatim. In the vast majority of cases, they cannot. As part of my yearlong academy (LACE), I ask them to write up their school and district mission, vision, and values statements, and to deconstruct them for how adequately they prioritize character development as a school or district outcome goal. Usually, there is little that is of direct and explicit relevance to character development and education. Some talk exclusively about academic achievement. For example, the mission of the St. Louis Public Schools is "We will provide a quality education for all students and enable them to realize their full intellectual potential." Their vision is "St. Louis Public Schools is the district of choice for families in the St. Louis region that provides a world-class education and is nationally recognized as a leader in student achievement and teacher quality." Others have tangentially related concepts like "lifelong learners" or "productive citizens," and think that specifically alludes to character development. One district recently adopted the mission statement that "we do whatever it takes to ensure all students realize their potential" and a vision that "by continuously improving in every aspect of our performance, the . . . District empowers students to command their future." Many of the schools in the district are adopting the district mission as a school mission. The principals of those schools tend to think the mission and vision statements represent character as a priority. Unfortunately, they do not. Realizing one's "potential" is not normative; one might have potential to be a great assassin or to cure cancer. Commanding one's future suffers from the same problem. From an ethical standpoint, not only is there no normative concept in either of these statements, but the opening phrase "we do whatever it takes" is a complete violation of the ethical principle that the ends do not justify the means. The real point here, however, is that principals (and other educators) usually do not even see the lack of prioritization in their own mission and vision statements.

The LACE exercise to deconstruct the statements typically requires two steps before the principals "get it." First, they present and, sometimes, reflect on the statements, but they do not see the lack of prioritization. Second, we provide constructive feedback and ask them to collaboratively reflect on our feedback with their character education leadership team. At this point, they are much more likely to begin to "get it." Underlying this malaise is the fact that most school leaders do not have a clear mission or vision for their schools. One principal countered this by actually writing up his educational philosophy and distributed it widely, not only to staff, but to parents and others. In fact, he sent it in advance to every job applicant so they would know the kind of school he was trying to lead. For most leaders, however, developing and articulating a mission, vision, educational philosophy, or long-term strategic plan is an unrealized but critical leadership task.

Karen Smith became principal of Mark Twain Elementary School in Brentwood, Missouri, in 2002. She had a long-term strategic plan, in part building upon her success at her previous school. She began with her staff: "[W]e began implementation in 2003–2004 with staff self-reflections." This was coupled with professional development. The next year, they joined a group of schools implementing Caring School Communities under the auspices of CHARACTERplus. Then, in the following year, they focused on family involvement ("parents were my biggest challenge in those early years") and service programs. In other words, this was a systematic long-term strategy. As Karen describes it, "we like little steps that are designed to institutionalize effective change!" As with the other exemplary schools cited in this chapter, the proof is clear. For example, their percentage of students scoring at the proficient or advanced level increased from 30 in 2005 to 75 in 2009. From 2003–2010, discipline referrals dropped by 79%, the number of students referred for discipline dropped by 77%, and bullying referrals dropped by over 75%. According to Karen, "The use of student self-reflection for inappropriate behaviors and natural consequences accounts for most of this change" (personal communication, 2010).

So, for most principals, at some point a light bulb has to go on as they "get it," i.e., as they recognize in a detailed and informed manner that the development of character of their students is a prime purpose of schooling, and that they, as the school leaders, have to be at the helm of that journey. I have seen this epiphany happen in many ways and for quite different reasons. Karen Smith was looking for a way to increase academic achievement at her previous school, Clearview Elementary in Washington, Missouri, and attended a presentation by the Developmental Studies Center about their Child Development Program. She came to realize that focusing on school climate and character might be the path to her academic goal, so she applied to LACE. What she learned was applied at Clearview and then at her subsequent school, Mark Twain Elementary, which has since been recognized as a Blue Ribbon School and a Missouri School of Character.

At some point a light bulb has to go on . . . as [principals] recognize . . . that the development of character of their students is a prime purpose of schooling, and that they, as the school leaders, have to be at the helm of that journey.

From a different angle, Amy Johnston, a highly accomplished middle school principal, felt that something was missing from making her job as head of a large suburban middle school fulfill the reasons she first entered the profession of education. She claims that an application for LACE mysteriously appeared on her desk and she decided to apply. LACE provided the vision for what a great school should be and lit a fire under her that has led to recognition of Francis Howell Middle School (St. Charles, MO) as a National School of Character and winner of the Partnership School Award, and their achievement scores have skyrocketed (e.g., 67% reduction in F grades from 2004 to 2010; state math scores are 25% higher and communication arts scores are 17% higher than the other four middle schools in the same district) while their misbehavior data have plummeted (e.g., in a school of approximately 850 students, detentions decreased from 1,153 in 2003 to 203 in 2010). These cases exemplify the two most common motivations to embrace quality character education, i.e., either because it is a means to greater and more robust academic success, or because it is fundamental to the mission of a school and an educator. School leaders need to "get" one or ideally both of these. Finding ways to help educators "get it" is so fundamental to my work as an educational consultant that I often think my title should be "Epiphany Engineer."

LEADING THE CHARGE: MAKING CHARACTER EDUCATION AN INSTITUTIONAL PRIORITY

No school reform initiative can thrive without the principal as its champion, and no successful initiative is principal-proof. An antagonistic principal can undo or at least do sustained damage to such an initiative. Character education needs a champion at the helm of the school. The Healthy School Communities initiative of the Association for Supervision and Curriculum Development (ASCD, 2010) has recently concluded that "the role of the principal was the most critical piece of the puzzle in implementing meaningful school change and school improvement" (p. 1) and that "planning teams should be principal-led" (p. 4). As Mark Eichenlaub, former principal of Jefferson Elementary in Belleville, IL (a National School of Character), said, "This is obvious for all of us, as building leaders: We were responsible for keeping the ship headed in the right direction. Never backing off what was best for kids set the tone for all activities." The question then is how do principals show commitment to and prioritization of character education?

ASCD (2010) has suggested one such means: serving on or, better yet, leading the school reform team. The first LACE assignment is to assemble a representative stakeholder character education team in the school. We urge the principal to serve on it and, when appropriate, to lead it. We also suggest that it be the overall school culture, school climate, and school improvement team. Putting character education in the driver's seat of school reform and seeing the principal actively engaged in this is one way to demonstrate its importance. I have (and many of you likely have as well) experienced failures in such leadership. I recall being invited by a lead teacher to present an after-school workshop in an urban high school some years back. It was my first visit to this school and I knew none of the staff. Apparently, I was to be part of the regular staff meeting. The principal first took care of some minor business, then introduced me . . . and left! My heart sank as I knew that my impact had just been severely compromised by the symbolic (and likely actual) disrespect of character education by the principal's glaring departure. Presence and participation speak loudly as indicators of a principal's commitment.

It is worth inserting a cautionary dichotomy here. I have discovered that there are two basic forms of delegation: authentic and inauthentic. Authentic delegation happens when a principal assigns the leadership authority to another. There are two core ingredients to authentic delegation. First, the principal truly believes that the delegate would be a good lead person for the initiative, project, or in this case character education effort. In some senses, this is a form of leadership mentoring; i.e., good principals look for leadership potential in others and proactively cultivate it. Amy Johnston, the principal of Francis Howell Middle School discussed above, has repeatedly nurtured leadership in her staff, and as a result, more than half a dozen of her former staff are principals or assistant principals in other schools. Brenda Logan, former principal of Hazelwood Elementary School, "encouraged staff to become leaders" and reports that over 15 "staff members have moved on to leadership positions . . . throughout the district." Steve Zwolak, director of University City Children's Center (a private inner-city early childhood center in Missouri), systematically trains administrative competencies and then sends those new leaders to lead their own schools. In fact, Steve invests heavily in professional development of his staff in general and in prospective leaders in particular. But when he mentors a future leader, his investment is publicly and explicitly tied to the desire for them not to stay in his school, as most would do, but rather to "go forth and multiply." All exemplary leaders, Steve, Brenda, and Amy authentically delegate to others, and they do so with the intention of emptying the nest. The second ingredient in authentic delegation is to intend to (and actually) "have the delegate's back." In other words, when there is pushback from staff, students, parents, and so forth, the principal will back up the delegate and lend his or her authority to whatever the delegate has proposed or requested. In addition, the principal will supply the necessary resources to allow the delegate to succeed.

Inauthentic delegation is when the principal assigns another to take on a task that he or she does not want and does not see as a true priority. I have seen this repeatedly in character education, most commonly in high schools, but across the PreK–12 spectrum. In most cases, there is external pressure on the principal to engage in character education (sometimes from the district administration), so the principal assigns an assistant principal, counselor, or lead teacher to "lead" the character education initiative. But all the principal is really interested in is (1) dumping the job on someone else and (2) being able to report that there is a character education initiative in the school. When the pushback comes, the principal does not back up the delegate, and when resources are needed, the principal does not provide them. This can be very harmful to morale and clearly frustrating to the often unwitting delegate who frequently thinks the inauthentic delegation is actually authentic. Furthermore, it is dishonest and cowardly.

A second way to demonstrate priority is through advocacy. When a principal serves as the town crier for character education, it demonstrates the importance it holds for him or her, and ultimately for the school. Over time, we have developed our "4W" model of how staff members often react to a new leader. The first W is that staff may think they can *wait out* the new principal. One of the staff in Amy Johnston's school said that when Amy first contracted character education fever, the staff person figured this would pass if she just waited for the heat to die down. Amy, as if reading her mind, said, "and don't think this will go away, because it won't." It didn't. So when staff members are waiting out the principal, the principal has two main alternatives: *Win over* the abstainers or *winnow out* the resistors. In fact, we recommend that they try to win over all the staff first and then ascertain which are true resistors who are not salvageable. Jennifer Reph, as the new principal of Tremont Elementary School in New York, discovered that the staff were waiting out her new character education initiative (and other innovations, most notably in literacy education), but she determined that they were good staff and so she worked hard and deliberately to win them over. Not only did she ultimately succeed (not one staff member left), but Tremont was recognized as a National School of Character in 2005 in large part for following her vision.

One of the most remarkable turnaround stories in the character education world is that of Ridgewood Middle School (RMS) in Arnold, Missouri, and its journey is quite different. Ridgewood (Haynes & Berkowitz, 2007) was a failing school. Only 9% of its students were meeting state academic standards, graffiti adorned all the bathroom walls and other surfaces, litter abounded, and student behavior and attendance were terrible. There were no resource officers (i.e., police assigned to the school) in any other district school, including the high schools, but there were two assigned to RMS. This school draws from a tough population with over 40% eligible for free and reduced lunch and most of the rest very close to eligibility. The school had long before become the district's dumping ground for tenured teachers that other principals did not want, so the staff was largely incompetent, burned out, outright antagonistic to students, or simply treading water. Then-superintendent Diana Bourisaw saw the problem and brought in a new leadership team to fix this failing school. Tim Crutchley (principal) and Kristen Pelster (assistant principal) began a campaign to articulate and enact a character education vision for the school. Most of the staff did not respond to the articulation, to the advocacy, nor to the modeling (including in the classrooms) by the new leaders. Ultimately, Crutchley offered an ultimatum in February of the first year, essentially saying that the school was going in this direction and that if staff did not want to join the journey, they should consider going elsewhere. At the end of that year, one-third of the staff left. After 3 years, two-thirds of the staff had left. Crutchley and Pelster were able to hire new staff who fit their vision. In 3 years, they were recognized as a National School of Character. Today, their percentage of students meeting state academic standards has risen from the abysmal 9% they inherited to 70%. A parallel improvement in student behavior was at the heart of the many recognitions RMS has received. In this case, winnowing out the naysayers was necessary for the school to succeed, and indeed, flourish.

Tim Crutchley (principal) and Kristen Pelster (assistant principal) began a campaign to articulate and enact a character education vision for the school. . . . In 3 years, they were recognized as a National School of Character. Today, their percentage of students meeting state academic standards has risen from the abysmal 9% they inherited to 70%.

The fourth and final W is to *work with the willing.* Every school, even a dumping ground for bad teachers like Ridgewood was, has some good teachers. When Tim Crutchley offered his ultimatum, he expected a pink slip the next day. Instead, what he got was about a third of the staff thanking him and saying they had been waiting for a leader with a positive vision. Finding the willing and working with them is critical. Brenda Logan (Hazelwood Elementary School) had 80% of her staff on board with the school initiative to implement the Child Development Project. There continued to be resistors, but "we didn't scorn/scold those staff members but just continued to move in the direction of becoming a caring school community." All too often, principals spend inordinate time on the unwilling (the obstructers and underminers), and forget what they learned in the classroom; i.e., they don't give the misbehavers the attention they are seeking. Oftentimes principals are so focused on the anticipated resistance that they change their desired messages, strategies, and priorities before ever sharing them with the staff (or other audiences). What they don't seem to realize is that they are giving inordinate power to the anticipated resistors; i.e., those people are impacting the principal's messages or strategies without the principal even knowing they are coming down the road!

A third means of setting priorities is to set, monitor, and enforce clear expectations. Simply saying what staff members are expected to do is not enough. We all quickly figure out what is enforced and authentically expected and what we can ignore. Jill Ramsey, recently retired as principal of Chesterfield Elementary in Missouri, a National School of Character, reported that

> my expectation became using class meetings to set norms and conducting them weekly to resolve climate issues. Teachers were expected to have class meetings in every classroom that year. I also had "conversational struggles" with those teachers

who were not buying into this approach of using student voice to positively affect climate. In a couple of cases, these conversations resulted in teachers leaving Chesterfield.

WALKING THE TALK

While the gist of setting the priority is to talk the walk (to be the town crier for character education as an institutional priority), an equally important task of the effective leader is to walk the talk, i.e., to be a role model. We must be the character we want to see in others and for principals, we must be the character educator that we want to see in our staff. In this sense, the principal is a role model in two broad ways. First, she must model the kind of pedagogy, behavior management, and so on that she wants her teachers to enact. Second, she must be the kind of person (have the character) that she wants her staff and students (and all other stakeholders) to be.

Being a paragon of virtue is certainly supererogatory. Most educators blanch at the thought of being held to such a high personal standard. Education is not and should not be merely a job. Rather, it is a calling, no less so than the calling to religious life or military service. It is a calling to service to others, and those others first and foremost are the students. Schools are there for students, not for the teachers or their unions, not for the parents or their votes, not for the administrators or their school boards. One helpful perspective on this is servant leadership (Greenleaf, 1991; Hunter, 1998). When a leader understands that his primary role is to serve his school and its stakeholders, then he is open to a path toward success. Pat McEvoy, new principal at Bayless (MO) High School, has said that his role is like a Hollywood producer. He notes that the true talent in Hollywood is the writer, director, actors, and so forth. The job of the producer is to get them the resources they need to do their jobs excellently. A principal's role is to provide the resources and context so the teachers and other staff can do their jobs optimally, so the students have the best chance at flourishing in school and in life outside of school. In a study of educational leadership development programs, Darling-Hammond and her colleagues (Darling-Hammond, Meyerson, LaPointe, & Orr, 2010) argued that the "ability to 'support the adults so that they can support the kids' is an in-a-nutshell description of instructional leadership" (p. 4). Greenleaf argued that "the secret of institution building is to be able to weld a team of . . . people by lifting them up to grow taller than they would otherwise be" (p. 35).

One of the clearest examples is the degree to which leaders invest in the professional development of their staff. As the title of the 2000 Neila Connors book indicates, *If You Don't Feed the Teachers They Eat the Students.* One of the primary ways of feeding teachers is serving their professional development. Jill Ramsey began "the journey at Chesterfield Elementary . . . by providing professional development by [the author of this chapter] to the staff on class meetings and buddy activities." When Amy Johnston began the Francis Howell Middle School journey, she serendipitously was given $20,000 in unexpended federal funding, but it had to be expended in a matter of weeks or it would be lost. She and I quickly crafted a way to invest the money in the professional development of her staff. She brought 17 people to my summer institute in character education (still the largest group ever to attend from one school), and her school was off and running. As a principal, do you make it easier for staff to be out of the building for quality professional development, to attend graduate classes, to access professional development funds, and so on? And do you model professional development yourself?

I suggested that they . . . (1) build healthy personal relationships with each teacher and (2) become a servant to their teachers. For the latter, I suggested they approach each teacher individually and ask, "What can I do to help you do your job better this year?"

At one middle school I have worked with, both the principal and assistant principal have graduated from LACE and are authentically and deeply committed to character education. However, they have not been successful in getting their teachers to buy in to this new vision. After pushing and pushing and getting more and more resistance, I offered them a new strategy. I suggested that they stop pushing character education and take a full year to do two things: (1) build healthy personal relationships with each teacher (more on this below); and (2) become a servant to their teachers. For the latter, I suggested they approach each teacher individually and ask, "What can I do to help you do your job better this year?" Of course, that comes with two catches: They have to authentically mean it, and they have to deliver (of course, within reason). They plan on starting the next school year this way, and I have high hopes for a breakthrough for them as leaders (I think this will be transformational for them), for their staff as potential character educators, and for the school in general.

Amy Johnston (principal of Francis Howell Middle School) reports that when they began their character education journey about 8 years ago, she suddenly realized that it implied that they would be held to the same standard as they were proposing for their students; in other words, they had to be respectful, responsible, caring, fair, honest, and so forth. That was a daunting realization but to her credit and that of her staff, they were willing to take on the challenge. Some of her staff (and teachers from many other schools) report that this journey made them not only better educators, but better people: better parents, better spouses, and so on. Rima Vesilind, former principal of Woodley Hills Elementary (a National School of Character in Virginia),

> modeled support for my staff by taking a family of five who were living in a car into my home—single mother and four children. That experience gave me a deeper understanding of what it was like to have nothing and to have to work through Social Services to support a family.

Many great principals understand, like Rima, that they cannot ask their staff to do things they themselves are not willing to do. When Tim Crutchley and Kristen Pelster, at RMS, discovered that so many students were failing because they were not handing in their work and teachers were assigning them zero grades for the missing work, they established a ZAP (Zeros Are not Permitted) program. Every day at lunch, there was a separate area for students who had missing work. But as good leaders they realized that they could not dump the responsibility for chasing down noncompliant students on teachers. Instead, they personally staffed 1.5 hours of this study hall every day. Once a teacher handed in the ZAP form, it was the principal's job to get the work done. They also routinely went to the homes of tardy students to drag them out of bed and get them to school. When Karen Smith and her counselor, Myra Earls, implemented the Navigator Buddy program at Mark Twain Elementary, each staff member volunteered to work with an at-risk student. The idea was to provide a special adult–child relationship for students who needed additional support while at school. Karen as principal had a Buddy, as did Karen's secretary, Marie. The power of this came into poignant clarity when Karen's fourth-grade Buddy was home over Spring Break with his older, special-needs brother when their father murdered their mother and then took his own life. This 10-year-old had Karen's cell number as her Buddy and could call her for help and support in the aftermath of this horrendous tragedy. "The advantage was the close relationship I had with [her Buddy] that helped me meet his needs and help family members (who I had never met) transition both boys into the new life they would be beginning."

Other principals have taught me that the best way to get students or staff to act in desired ways is for the principal to model it. Janis Wiley, former principal at Mann Elementary in St. Louis, reported that she got the students to pick up litter in the school yard simply by going out each day and doing so herself. Mike Galvin, former principal of Columbine Elementary School in Colorado (2000 National School of Character), wanted a school where

> everyone took responsibility for all the students (not just those in their own class, or those under their care at specific times of the day). The idea was to spread leadership around a bit—trying to build an ethic based on Peter Block's definition of leadership as "taking responsibility for the good of the whole."

He especially wanted shared responsibility applied to students with special needs, i.e., a mix of inclusion and shared leadership/responsibility. As with Janis, who needed to do the "dirty work" so that students would do likewise, Mike had to do the dirty work to get the staff to do so.

> One boy, a fourth grader with severe cerebral palsy, had problems with bowel control and often had to be cleaned up by whoever was available. After hearing a few times, "Well,

that's not MY job" or "I'm too busy," I let the teachers and teacher assistants know I was available for diapering and clean up duty and insisted they call on me. Of course, it only took one or two times of me doing cleanup for the message to get across: We all pitch in, wherever and whenever we can help.

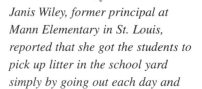

Janis Wiley, former principal at Mann Elementary in St. Louis, reported that she got the students to pick up litter in the school yard simply by going out each day and doing so herself.

The other part of role modeling is being the character education instructional leader and more generally a model of the practices that they want their staff to implement. One of my pet peeves is faculty meetings. I take perverse pleasure in reenacting what such meetings typically look like. When I do that, it sadly looks quite familiar to most educators. Some of the problems with the typical routine of a set of announcements read by the principal to the staff are that (1) all of their staff are literate and could have read all that material outside of the meeting, (2) they are wasting the only time the staff gets together as a community when they could have been strategically building the adult community, and (3) they are modeling terrible pedagogy. My recommendation is to sit in a circle and simply talk about how to make the school a better place for everyone. As Gus Jacob, former principal of one of Ernest Boyer's original Basic Schools, has said, "when teachers talk to teachers about teaching, good things happen for children." I would add that when principals talk *with* (not *to*) teachers about teaching, then good things happen for students because the principals are modeling collaborative, democratic, constructivist pedagogy. Amy Johnston (Francis Howell Middle School) likes to ask provocative questions, which she refers to as "starting World War III"—for example, "How do we handle late work?" "How many Fs did we give last semester? Why? And when and why do we give zeros and how can that philosophy reflect true learning of the curriculum?" "What is the difference between teaching and learning?" These lead to great discussions and help move an adult culture (and a school) forward, which as we saw above is the core of John Dewey's (1909) definition of morality and the moral purpose of schools.

Another innovation Amy Johnston made was to replace most whole-staff meetings with plan-time meetings of smaller groups. The idea was that the staff was pretty large and those large meetings were not the best use of their time. So instead she meets with smaller groups during shared plan time. As Amy reports, "they aren't class meetings, but they give the same feel because everyone is heard and each meeting is different because the [participants] are different" at each meeting. This, then, becomes the leader modeling both self-sacrifice (spending more time in meetings) and good pedagogy (a form of class meetings). The teachers union actually tried to stop her school from doing these plan-time meetings, but the staff so valued them that they continue to do them anyhow.

Mark Eichenlaub established a schoolwide morning meeting for Jefferson Elementary in Belleville, Illinois, as a fulcrum for school improvement.

> The daily meeting started every day with the Jefferson family together, setting the tone for the day's activities. It focused all on the single vision of building an environment through developing a single vision. Of everything I had to do as a principal, I rarely missed my daily meeting with the students. I made it a top priority.

For him, this was also the modeling of how to lead class meetings.

> I kicked off the school year by personally leading a school-wide class meeting of K–sixth graders, approximately 400 students. In doing this, I was able to model the power of effective class meetings. Staff was able to see that even first graders were able to grow and were willing to participate.

HUMAN RESOURCES EXPERT

One of the biggest challenges for school leaders is the strategic and intentional management of adult human resources. I was on an airplane heading home and chatting with my row mate. When he learned that I do character education, he said, "My partner and I are in real estate. In real estate, there are 3 Ls: location, location,

location. But I used to be in private loan banking, and we had 3 Cs: credit, collateral, character. But I think it should be character, character, character." When I asked why, he said, "if you loan money to someone with poor character, I don't care how rich they are, they are going to try to avoid paying you back. And if you loan money to someone with good character, I don't care how poor they are, they are going to eventually find a way to pay you back." That is when the light bulb went on for me. And I said, "you know the three Rs of education, reading, 'riting, and 'rithmatic? Well, the three Rs of character education are relationships, relationships, relationships." I just discovered that James Comer similarly wrote, in 1999, "*Children's . . . development* depends on *relationships*. I have often said that relationships are to development what location is to real estate: We need relationship, relationship, relationship" (p. xxiv, italics original).

The key point is that not only child development, but child learning, and the institutional culture upon which they both depend, rely upon healthy, prosocial relationships. Schools need to systematically and intentionally foster such relationships. Certainly the principal needs to "get," prioritize, and model this. But she also needs to be the social engineer for the adult culture. This is something that is not taught in most educational leadership programs, or certainly not in the depth necessary for optimal performance in a school leadership role. Brenda Logan, former principal at Hazelwood Elementary School (Louisville, KY), reports that, at her hiring in 1990, her then superintendent said, "Brenda, you would not have made it to his point in the application process without being knowledgeable about a lot of areas that a principal is responsible for. From this point on, however, what will matter most is how you deal with people." Principals often stumble because they don't know how to adjudicate conflicts between teachers (or other staff) or between teachers and parents. They don't know how to deal with resistors. They are not prepared to handle a teacher who is in meltdown because her husband left her that morning, for example. Principals need to recognize that it is their job to deal with intrapersonal and interpersonal crises and to proactively build a positive adult community and culture. One place this has been dealt with effectively is in the social-emotional learning literature (Patti & Tobin, 2003). Research supports the argument that the principal as the central player in an ethical and caring adult community in the school, one where interpersonal trust reigns, is important for the school's effectiveness (Bryk & Schneider, 2002; Tschannen-Moran, 2004).

There are many strategies and tasks involved here. One is staff selection. Hiring staff members who share the same educational philosophy and vision makes it more likely that the staff will gel and form a cohesive culture. Rima Vesilind reports that when she became principal of West Potomac High School, "I hired staff who cared about students and who believed that character development was the core of all instruction." As noted above, when Kristen Pelster and Tim Crutchley took over leadership of RMS, two-thirds of the staff left after 3 years. This afforded them the opportunity to hire staff who resonated with their vision for the school.

Another strategy is having the courageous conversations with those who are resisting or undermining the welfare of the school. Mark Eichenlaub (Jefferson Elementary School) reports that

> I had two teachers who were not in favor of doing character education. I met with them personally and listened to their concerns. Once that was done respectfully, and that was key, I let them know that the school and community had made a decision to move forward and they had three choices: come along on the journey, go to a different school, or resign. Glad to say they stayed and ended up being two of the greatest champions of character on staff. As a leader, your staff deserves that honest yet respectful dialogue, as it can make a difference for the character education movement and their careers.

Such conversations don't have to be one on one. Amy Johnston (Francis Howell Middle School) had to confront the same issue that Pelster and Crutchley faced, namely too many failing grades due to unsubmitted homework. While Pelster and Crutchley went to each teacher and asked him or her to explain each failing grade, Johnston charted the grades and distributed the list of all teachers and all the failing grades to the entire teaching staff. She simply asked them what they saw in the data and let them come to their own conclusions. This discussion led to a zero-tolerance policy for zero grades, similar to what happened at Ridgewood Middle.

Fundamentally, leaders who can build strong relationships are adept at putting the "self" on hold. This is a highly complex skill that takes years to perfect. Allowing oneself to be the conduit that seeks and elicits more and more trust from the other, without inserting your own agenda, gives the other person the space to fill, while giving him or her the needed social permission to do so. Such leaders also need to have a shared willingness with others to engage in authentic and transparent exchanges. To do so, they also need self-knowledge and the willingness and openness to share feelings and thoughts with others.

Underlying all this is that principals need to treat staff the way they want staff to treat others, just as we have already discussed above in the section on modeling.

A Pedagogy of Empowerment

If schools are to promote character, and if they are to promote the development of future democratic citizens (Berman, 1997), they must be democratic themselves. Sadly, the entire American education system is woefully hierarchical and authoritarian (Wagner & Kegan, 2006). While I frequently promote a pedagogy of empowerment in the classroom (e.g., class meetings, shared norms, cooperative learning, etc.), it is also imperative for principals to parallel that in the way they run their schools. They need to be willing and able to share leadership (Deal & Peterson, 2009). In a sense, this is an example of the leadership paradox; i.e., how can one lead by giving up control, by sharing one's authority and responsibility with others?

One of the biggest wastes of resources in schools is the disuse of the minds of students and teachers. Students, even kindergartners, will often outthink their teachers. Likewise, teachers will often outthink their administrators. Yet all too rarely do teachers ask students to solve problems, make decisions, plan events, and so on. And all too rarely do principals ask teachers to do likewise. Principals need to flatten the governance structures in the school, empower staff and other stakeholders, and simply make intentional and institutionalized space in schools for all those voices

"Seeing that our test scores in math were suffering primarily in the African American male population, I asked a group of successful junior and senior Black males for their ideas. They . . . worked with me to create a mentorship group, BAM— Brothers Achieving More—that raised math scores of Black males and positively changed the culture of that population."

to be aired, to be heard, and to matter (Barth, 2001).

Rima Vesilind reports that at both her schools, this was a priority. At Woodley Hills Elementary, "I led a community retreat—4 half-days during which every staff member, many parents, and several interested community members participated—to determine our core values, our concerns, and suggestions for change." At West Potomac High, her focus was on empowering students:

> I got students to help. Seeing that our test scores in math were suffering primarily in the African American male population, I asked a group of successful junior and senior Black males for their ideas. They were shocked at the data and worked with me to create a mentorship group, BAM—Brothers Achieving More—that raised math scores of Black males and positively changed the culture of that population.

Kristen Pelster claims that the biggest influence on the culture and success of RMS was "creating and implementing character/ leadership classes for students that empowered *all* students to lead and created autonomy and a sense of belonging in the school."

Empowerment was a cornerstone of the success at Hazelwood Elementary School. Brenda Logan, former principal, reports that "my belief in collaborative decision making, involving the entire staff in school reform and 'thinking' that I could work with all people was the foundation for moving into that first year." This, for her, was the "principle that became a basis for success." As a school leader, it was her understanding the strategic (and ethical) importance of respect for and empowerment of others that buttressed the growth at Hazelwood. "I have always looked for strengths in other people that would serve as positive contributions to whatever initiative we were working on and to be inclusive of other people's thoughts and opinions, even when very different from my own."

CONCLUSION

Schools must be places not only of academic learning but also of student development, particularly of the development of moral and civic character. School leadership is the single most critical element in whether and how well this happens. While we do not have a lot of research on the nature and impact of school leadership in creating schools of character, we have enough to know that such leaders need to understand this basic thesis (to "get" it); need to make it an authentic priority for the school; need to model it in how they act personally and professionally; need to be an intentional and effective social engineer in promoting a caring and ethical culture among staff first and then among all stakeholders; and need to foster and model a pedagogy of empowerment where all stakeholders' voices are given space, are heard, and make a difference. Some may be tempted to argue that this is not unique to character education leadership, that rather, this is simply good educational leadership. I don't disagree at all. I often say that good character education is good education. Likewise, good character education leadership is simply good educational leadership. Investing in such good leadership, through selection and professional development, is investing in our schools, our children, and ultimately our future.

REFERENCES

Association for Supervision and Curriculum Development. (2010). *Learning, teaching, and leading in healthy school communities.* Alexandria, VA: Author.

Barth, R. S. (2001). *Learning by heart.* San Francisco: Jossey-Bass.

Benninga, J. S., Berkowitz, M. W., Kuehn, P., & Smith, K. (2003). The relationship of character education implementation and academic achievement in elementary schools. *Journal of Research in Character Education, 1,* 19–32.

Berkowitz, M. W., & Bier, M. C. (2005). *What works in character education: A research-driven guide for educators.* Washington, DC: Character Education Partnership.

Berkowitz, M. W., & Puka, B. (2009). Dissent and character education. In M. Gordon (Ed.), *Reclaiming dissent: Civic education for the 21st century* (pp. 107–130). Amsterdam: Sense Publishers.

Berman, S. (1997). *Children's social consciousness and the development of social responsibility.* Albany: State University of New York Press.

Boyer, E. L. (1995). *The Basic School: A community for learning.* Princeton, NJ: Carnegie Foundation for the Advancement of Teaching.

Bryk, A. S., & Schneider, B. (2002). *Trust in schools: A core resource for improvement.* New York: Russell Sage Foundation.

Comer, J. P. (1999). Child by child: The Comer process for change in education. In J. P. Comer, M. Ben-Avie, N. M. Haynes, & E. T. Joyner (Eds.), *Child by child: The Comer process for change in education* (pp. xix–xxvii). New York: Teachers College Press.

Conners, N. A. (2000). *If you don't feed the teachers they eat the students.* Nashville, TN: Incentive Publications.

Darling-Hammond, L., Meyerson, D., LaPointe, M., & Orr, M. T. (2010). *Preparing principals for a changing world: Lessons from effective school leadership programs.* San Francisco: Jossey-Bass.

Deal, T. E., & Peterson, K. D. (2009). *Shaping school culture: Pitfalls, paradoxes, & promises* (2nd ed.). San Francisco: Jossey-Bass.

Dewey, J. (1909). *Moral principles in education.* Boston: Houghton Mifflin.

Durkheim, E. (1961). *Moral education: A study in the theory and application of the sociology of education.* New York: The Free Press.

Feinberg, W. (1990). The moral responsibility of public schools. In J. I. Goodlad, R. Soder, & K. A. Sirotnik (Eds.), *The moral dimensions of teaching* (pp. 155–187). San Francisco: Jossey-Bass.

Greenleaf, R. K. (1991). *The servant as leader.* Westfield, IN: Greenleaf Center for Servant Leadership.

Haynes, C. C., & Berkowitz, M. W. (2007, February 20). What can schools do? *USA Today,* p. 13a.

Hunter, J. C. (1998). *The servant: A simple story about the true essence of leadership.* Roseville, CA: Prima.

Jackson, P. W., Boostrom, R. E., & Hansen, D. T. (1993). *The moral life of schools.* San Francisco: Jossey-Bass.

Kohlberg, L., & Mayer, R. (1972). Development as the aim of education: The Dewey view. *Harvard Educational Review, 42,* 449–496.

McCabe, D. L. (1999). Academic dishonesty among high school students. *Adolescence, 34,* 681–687.

Patti, J., & Tobin, J. (2003). *Smart school leaders: Leading with emotional intelligence.* Dubuque, IA: Kendall/Hunt.

Payton, J., Weissberg, R. P., Durlak, J. A., Dymnicki, A. B., Taylor, R. D., Schellinger, K.B., et al. (2008). *The positive impact of social and emotional learning for kindergarten to eighth-grade students.* Chicago: Collaborative for Academic, Social, and Emotional Learning.

Power, F. C., Higgins, A., & Kohlberg, L. (1989). *Lawrence Kohlberg's approach to moral education.* New York: Columbia University Press.

Sizer, T. R., & Sizer, N. F. (1999). *The students are watching: Schools and the moral contract.* Boston: Beacon Press.

Sockett, H. (1993). *The moral base for teacher professionalism.* New York: Teachers College Press.

Tschannen-Moran, M. (2004). *Trust matters: Leadership for successful school.* San Francisco: Jossey-Bass.

Wagner, T., & Kegan, R. (2006). *Change leadership: A practical guide to transforming our schools.* San Francisco: Jossey-Bass.

CHAPTER SIX

LEADING FOR SOCIAL RESPONSIBILITY

SHELDON H. BERMAN

In 1981, I helped found a new national organization focused on assisting schools in teaching social responsibility. I was a high school social studies teacher at the time and observed the painful level of disengagement and alienation my students felt from the social and political world around them. They sensed that individuals had little voice in the political arena or power to influence change. I had entered teaching because I enjoyed working with young people and thought of teaching as one of the best ways I could help the next generation realize that they could make a difference in the world through their daily actions at home and through their future work, no matter where they chose to live or what profession they chose to enter. I attempted to help them overcome this sense of disempowerment through the classes I taught. In some cases, I was quite successful. However, I realized that the problem was not going to be solved by one or even a group of passionately committed social studies teachers. Any meaningful awakening of civic engagement would require a systemically different approach to education in which social responsibility framed the core mission.

Social responsibility in the form of civic engagement has historically been the core mission of American education. The concept of educating for effective citizenship is a theme we can trace among educational leaders throughout our national history, from Thomas Jefferson to Horace Mann, and from John Dewey to John Goodlad. Literacy and numeracy were promoted not only for professional success, but also to develop an educated citizenry that could make intelligent public policy choices and preserve a democratic republic. These educational leaders did not want the public to be fooled by demagogues or to fall prey to simple answers for complex problems.

For some, such as Francis Parker and John Dewey, the primary mission of education was the advancement of social justice and social reform. Dewey, in his extraordinary 1897 essay entitled "My Pedagogic Creed," asserted,

> I believe that education is the fundamental method of social progress and reform. I believe that all reforms which rest simply upon the enactment of law, or the threatening of certain penalties, or upon changes in mechanical or outward arrangements, are transitory and futile. (p. 80)

He added that, "social consciousness is the only sure method of social reconstruction" (p. 80). In his 1916 work, *The Need for an Industrial Education in an Industrial Society*, he took this further, saying that "democracy must be born anew every generation, and education is its midwife" (quoted in Dewey, 2008, p. 139).

That larger mission for education has been the inspiration for my life's work. If we are to create a more just, peaceful, and sustainable world, how can we do it unless we help our young people cultivate a sense of social consciousness and a commitment to making their world a better place? Forming that sense of social consciousness and social responsibility doesn't just happen. It takes intention, attention, and time. It is what education is all about, and it lends meaning to the study of the other disciplines, including math, science, the arts, literature, and social studies. The heart of education is enabling and encouraging young people to apply the knowledge and skills they are developing—not merely for their *own* success and satisfaction, but to serve the common good.

LEADERSHIP FOR SOCIAL JUSTICE

The heart of education is enabling and encouraging young people to apply the knowledge and skills they are developing—not merely for their own success and satisfaction, but to serve the common good.

For me, social responsibility has meant assisting students to make a personal investment in the well-being of others and the planet. It has entailed helping them develop a sense of social consciousness and a commitment to making the world a better place for their having participated in it. Over the past 30 years— initially providing organizational leadership for Educators for Social Responsibility as we worked with schools to make social responsibility core to the curriculum, and then through 17 years as superintendent in two very different districts—I have learned a great deal about both the challenges and strategies of providing leadership that moves social responsibility, a concern for social justice, and the belief in democratic participation forward.

The lesson that stands out most is the importance of a leader grasping this larger purpose, articulating it for all staff, and maintaining a focus on it through even the toughest of organizational issues. As administrators, we get mired in day-to-day struggles, crises, and challenges. Academic accountability looms large over everything with its myopic focus on the basics of math, reading, and—tangentially—science. Too often, it promotes academics without meaning, performance without purpose, knowledge without context. It is tough to teach in such an environment, and it is equally difficult to lead when you are facing the harsh consequences of state and federal sanctions. We get so entangled in the intricacies of accountability that we lose all sense of purpose and meaning in our work. However, it is that sense of meaning and purpose that motivates people to do great work, to go beyond what is expected, and to achieve wondrous things. Most teachers and administrators enter the profession because they care deeply about children and want to make a difference. Connecting them back to the deeper purposes of our profession, their importance to our society, and the civic mission that drives education, serves to enhance their self-esteem and inspires them to identify with the larger mission of the district.

Too often, we are warned that if we take our eye off of reading and math to pay attention to social responsibility, we will see standardized test scores falter. In actuality, just the opposite occurs. Academic achievement is critically linked to school and classroom culture, to student engagement, and to students' sense of meaning in their studies. What I have found is that by structuring reform to focus on each of these elements in a way that enhances social responsibility, students' academic performance increases—as does their investment in their learning and their sense of connection to their school.

That a leader cares enough to make social justice and social responsibility a priority is a powerful statement to staff. It is a statement of conviction and courage in the face of great challenges. Students clearly need to become highly proficient readers and writers and to develop a solid understanding of how to use the number system. These skills are important and basic to all that we do. However, they should be recognized and promulgated not as ends in themselves, but as tools that serve to promote a better understanding of subjects of significance.

David Pierson, Dean of the College of Education at the University of California-Berkeley, visited Louisville, Kentucky, to participate in a team that was assessing our school district's reading program. In a debriefing dinner with key members of the superintendent's cabinet, he posed a very different perspective on the study of reading and math. He suggested that there are only two subjects worthy of study: science, because it is the study of the way *the world* works, and social studies, because it is the study of the way *people* work in the world. All the other content areas are tools to further the study of those two subjects. We debated the role of the arts as a subject or as a vehicle of communication. However, there is much truth in David's iconoclastic statement. Our goal in education must be to help students understand the way the world works and their role in it. It is only through the clarity of vision and the articulate focus of educational leaders that we can aspire to that larger mission.

The venues for communicating that vision present themselves not only in the significant traditions within a district—the opening day ceremonies, professional development sessions, graduations, and closing day ceremonies—but also in the daily and spontaneous moments of interaction with faculty and administrators. Staff members notice what administrators pay attention to, what we comment about in the artwork along the hallways, what we acknowledge in our congratulatory messages, how we justify our decisions, which student activities we celebrate and attend. In so many large and small ways, we make daily statements about what is important. People notice when we affirm students who have been civically engaged or performed a significant service-learning project. They notice when we encourage the faculty to devote class time to viewing important national events on television. They notice when we set priorities that ensure quality instruction in social studies or in social-emotional learning. If social responsibility, social justice, and civic engagement are important values, leaders need to live that vision and communicate to others how it frames all the work we do to enable young people to graduate as contributing members of our social and political community.

It is essential that a leader cares deeply about social responsibility and social justice and has a vision of how to breathe life into those values in the school setting. Yet, if that vision is to be realized, it must be firmly embedded in the mission of the district. In Hudson Public Schools, in Massachusetts, our collaboratively developed mission statement read,

Our goal is to promote the intellectual, ethical, civic, and social development of students through a challenging instructional program and a caring classroom and school environment.

That mission statement encompassed so much more than the traditional focus on academic success and specifically pointed to the importance of ethical, civic, and social development in our work. It also made clear that we must be as conscious of the culture of our classrooms as we are of their challenge level.

The Jefferson County Public Schools (JCPS) in Louisville developed a "Theory of Action" to guide its change and improvement efforts. This statement is an "if . . . then" or "when . . . then" declaration that identifies what results we want to achieve and what actions we are relying on to produce those results. That statement reads,

When we collaborate to

- *Create caring and culturally responsive classroom communities;*
- *Provide high-quality, personalized instruction that challenges and engages students in authentic work;*
- *Ensure equitable access for all students to a consistent, world-class, inquiry-based curriculum; and*
- *Prepare leaders to engage in collaborative strategies to move this shared vision forward . . .*

Then—
All students graduate with

- *A high level of academic performance;*
- *Strong character development and civic engagement; and*
- *Enhanced health and wellness . . .*

So that—
All students are prepared to

- *Achieve their goals;*
- *Follow their dreams; and*
- *Create a more just society.*

This theory of action was developed collaboratively over an extended period of time among the leadership of the district, reflecting the shared vision we bring to our work in education. It gathers under one philosophical umbrella, that which we know works best to facilitate powerful learning experiences for young people, as well as the kind of culture we need to create in our schools. But most important, it broadens our overarching goals to encompass character development and civic engagement, student health, and the commitment to creating a more just society. Because it is a theory of action, it guides all the strategic goals and initiatives in the district and frames the daily work we do.

In essence, embedding social justice into the guiding vision and mission documents of a school district is an essential element in communicating to staff members and the community that the work of the district has larger social meaning.

VISION IS NOT ENOUGH

Leadership for social justice and democracy involves more than believing in and articulating a vision, however. It means providing the leadership for integrating into the culture of schools and into classroom instruction those programs that effectively engender social responsibility and develop social consciousness.

At a foundational level, such leadership entails helping young people develop the social skills necessary to resolve conflicts and to problem solve with others. Often, our students come to school with very little experience in the basic social skills of greeting others appropriately, listening, acknowledging others, recognizing emotions, or taking the perspective of another person. Although teachers insist on respectful conduct, we tend to control that conduct through external rules and discipline codes. There are other, far more effective approaches that engage students in building a sense of community in the classroom, which in turn promotes an intrinsic motivation to support others.

Although teachers insist on respectful conduct, we tend to control that conduct through external rules and discipline codes. There are other, far more effective approaches that engage students in building a sense of community in the classroom, which in turn promotes an intrinsic motivation to support others.

In addition, the social and political world is often characterized by conflict in perspectives, political philosophies, conceptions of justice, and potential solutions to pressing social issues. Even at the local level, there is often controversy about which solutions will work best to address problems and improve the quality of life in a community. The two essential skills necessary to negotiate these conflicts and find mutually agreeable solutions are the ability to take the perspective of another and the ability to find common ground among competing positions.

In Jefferson County and in Hudson (the districts where I've served as superintendent), we initiated comprehensive social development programs to teach students basic social skills and nurture a caring sense of community in the classroom and school. These programs are not homegrown but rather are built on the rich experience and effective professional development provided by organizations such as the Developmental Studies Center, the Northeast Foundation for Children, Educators for Social Responsibility, the Committee for Children, and Origins.

In JCPS, we call this initiative CARE for Kids. Students experience and form critical social skills through a set of meetings purposely designed to foster community in the classroom. In most of our K–8 classrooms, students begin each day with morning meetings in which they greet each other, share experiences in their lives, listen carefully to others, discuss the agenda for the day, and build relationships with their classmates. These meetings provide focus and connection for students, particularly those whose lives are chaotic and challenged. In Grades K–5, students end each day with brief closing meetings in which they reflect on their day and share something that stood out for them, something they learned, or something that someone did to help another. Because community cannot exist unless students feel they have a voice and can make a difference in their classroom, teachers hold regular class meetings focused on solving class problems or making decisions and choices among options. These meetings provide students with significant opportunities to learn democratic decision-making skills and to develop strong bonds with other students as well as with the adults in the classroom.

These meetings are at times supplemented by peer mentoring programs between older and younger students, by schoolwide community-building programs, and by home–school activities that engage parents actively in the school community. Even the discipline system in these classrooms is designed so that infractions lead to appropriate consequences that promote self-reflection, restitution, and social skill development. These kinds of interactions enable students to construct positive relationships with peers and adults and to develop social and conflict resolution skills. However, what is actually most important is that students experience what it is like to be a responsible member of a community. Gradually, they arrive at the realization that their action, or lack of action, has an impact on others around them and on the quality of life in the community. Over time, they accept far greater responsibility for the smooth functioning of the classroom and the development of positive relationships.

One of the tensions in implementing a comprehensive social development program is that it takes time. Initially, this activity appears to take time away from instruction. Over the long term, however, it has precisely the opposite impact. Because students are better able to work together and resolve differences, there are fewer discipline issues in the classroom, fewer disruptions, and a far greater efficiency and productivity in cooperative and collaborative classroom activities and projects. Not surprisingly, the data analysis we have done in JCPS has shown that attendance improves and tardiness declines because students don't want to miss the important and productive social time with their classmates.

In addition, programs in social development are absolutely critical to the smooth and effective functioning of the inquiry-based curriculum programs in math and science that so many districts have adopted. Inquiry-based programs are designed to build student engagement and interest, and they make extensive use of group work and group problem solving. The skills students acquire through a social development program enable teachers to more effectively use these curricula and assist students to gain the conceptual benefit these programs are designed to offer. In terms of producing strong academic results, the social curricula of the classroom and school are as essential as the academic curriculum. We need to be forthright and intentional in our efforts to create positive, caring, and culturally responsive classrooms that enable students to feel safe, to feel connected to others, and to take risks so that they are better able to learn not only social responsibility, but also the content of the curriculum.

One of the other tensions in developing a caring classroom community is the challenge of creating what in JCPS we refer to as a culturally responsive classroom. Most teachers and other educators are the product of middle-class homes. Very few have personal experience with being evicted from their apartment or with racial profiling or with not understanding the language they hear spoken around them. Yet these are the types of background experiences some of our students bring to the classroom every day and have in the backs of their minds as we ask them to focus on curricular content. The problem is not that teachers do not care; it's that they simply haven't had experience with the wide variation in cultures that populate our schools today, and they may not be sensitive to ways of interacting with these students that would better encourage them to respond positively to school.

By "culture," I mean much more than just race; the term *culture* encompasses such issues as gender, country of origin, socioeconomics, faith, and customs. To create a bridge that supports student success for all students, JCPS has undertaken a systemic effort to promote cultural competence. Through a series of workshops and institutes, teachers, administrators, and support staff are engaging in activities and candid discussions that help them confront stereotypes and prejudices. As they come to understand lifestyles that may differ from their own, our employees become sensitive to students' everyday lives and are less apt to make unfounded assumptions about why some children respond in less-than-appropriate ways. Cultural competence training is assisting teachers to tie students' cultures directly to the curriculum and to the community, thereby helping children to feel safe and respected within the school setting and laying the groundwork for those same children to act in a socially responsible way toward others.

Creating an environment in the classroom and school that provides students with an experience of community, teaches them social skills, honors their culture, and models social problem solving is the foundation for students' developing a sense of social responsibility.

SELECTING CURRICULA TO SUPPORT STUDENT ENGAGEMENT

Engagement is the key to motivation and learning. Over the past two decades, educators have moved significantly away from didactic instruction based on textbooks and toward curricula designed around essential questions and interesting problems that promote conceptual development. At the heart of this shift is an understanding that learning is best promoted through intrinsic motivation, and that intrinsic motivation is best promoted by student engagement. However, the shift to student engagement is also critical for the development of social responsibility because it encourages and supports active participation in and ownership of learning. It moves students from a role as passive recipients of a "right answer" model of instruction to one in which students have to make decisions among multiple—and at times competing— answers to a problem. In this way, it brings their social and conflict resolution skill development into the academic arena.

Some of the best examples of curricula that promote engagement are in math and science where the National Science Foundation has invested millions of dollars in the development, pilot testing, refinement, and production of a number of outstanding programs. Common among such programs—including Investigations in Number, Data, and Space; Everyday Math; the Connected Mathematics Project; College Preparatory Mathematics; the Full Option Science System (FOSS); Science and Technology for Children (STC); and many others—is an inquiry-based model of instruction that engages students in questioning and problem solving.

Other curricula are also becoming available that blend academics with social development. The Developmental Studies Center has produced a powerful reading comprehension program entitled Making Meaning, as well as a writing program entitled Being a Writer, both of which teach social skills while developing students' comprehension and writing abilities.

These inquiry-based programs teach students how to think critically, collaborate more effectively, and problem solve—all basic skills in the development of social responsibility. However, helping students develop an understanding of social justice means directly engaging them in curricula that enhance their content knowledge of the social and political world, while giving them an opportunity to directly explore issues of social justice and civic engagement. There are numerous science, environmental, art, technology, and social studies curricula that can provide vehicles for the development of this understanding.

In social studies, for example, the Facing History and Ourselves Foundation has developed a profound civics curriculum entitled Facing History and Ourselves that explores the issue of intolerance through case studies of the

The curriculum complicates students' thinking so that they won't fall prey to simple answers and propaganda. It encourages students to avoid being bystanders when it comes to injustice and, instead, to profess a commitment to being "upstanders" for justice.

Holocaust and Armenian genocide. By exploring the essential question of how genocide can become state policy, students learn a great deal about history—but also about the conditions that lead to prejudice and social injustice and about the role of the individual in society. The curriculum complicates students' thinking so that they won't fall prey to simple answers and propaganda. It encourages students to avoid being bystanders when it comes to injustice and, instead, to profess a commitment to being "upstanders" for justice. In both Jefferson County and Hudson, this curriculum became the cornerstone of a civics curriculum required of all high school freshmen. The course provides a solid grounding in the basics of civics and government, as well as a deeper understanding of the meaning of social justice. However, its impact extends deep into the life of the classroom and the school by helping students understand that their school is truly a community and that they share in the responsibility to promote justice among students and adults in the school. Whether that means speaking out when a student uses a racial slur, or stepping in to make adults aware of a bullying situation, or simply actively promoting community engagement within the school and service outside the school, students begin to understand that their voices and their actions truly make a difference.

JCPS is now developing an elementary social studies curriculum that lays the foundation for civic understanding and engagement. Focusing on the three intertwined concepts of community, culture, and civics, the content at each grade level is designed around an essential question that supports the development of an appreciation for diversity within a community and an understanding of how individuals and organizations have made, and are making, a difference. The focus for kindergarten and first grade is on creating community from diversity. Children learn about the different cultures represented in their classroom and how people with different backgrounds and skills live together in a community. In second grade, students study a variety of cultures and countries around the world that reflect the cultures present in Louisville. They learn about two countries from each of four areas of the world, for example, Sudan and Nigeria in Africa— two countries from which new immigrants are arriving in Louisville. Through the study of community and culture, our youngest students are grounded in an understanding of the important role that individuals play in a community and how diversity offers us rich opportunities for learning.

The third-grade program teaches civics on a local and state level while children study local and state history. The essential question that students focus on is, "How do people make effective and responsible community decisions and improvements that benefit the common good?" As a result, students develop foundational knowledge in how our local and state governments work, as well as how individuals and organizations make a difference in our community. Students also study and work with an organization that is effectively tackling an issue; through this service-learning experience, they are introduced to the diversity of ways people can make a difference.

Fourth-grade students investigate the evolution of our political society through the lens of the development of civil and human rights. The essential question for fourth grade is, "What has enabled the United States to overcome obstacles and past history in order to expand the civil and human rights of people in the U.S.?" Through the study of the history of religious liberty; civil rights; women's suffrage; and the expansion of rights for disabled, immigrant, and homeless children and adults in the last half-century, children learn that civic participation of individuals and organizations has been critical in the expansion of civil and human rights in the United States. Simultaneously, they expand and refine their understanding of justice.

The fifth grade continues this study through the essential question, "How can we realize the democratic vision of all people participating in governmental decision making?" Students study the formation of the Constitution and the evolution of participatory democracy in the early years of the Republic. They then study the expansion of the right to vote and our national political structures and processes and learn about the importance of civic engagement as a way to make a difference in our community. The year culminates with their participation in *Project Citizen,* a curriculum developed by the Center for Civic Education that engages students in identifying, understanding, and making a difference on a local or state public policy issue. The year of focus on the evolution of the democratic process provides students with a deeper understanding of the concept of justice and its continuing permutations and refinements throughout our nation's history.

Undergirding the curriculum for all of the grades is a set of seven civic dispositions—commitment to social justice, compassion, critical mindedness, promotion of the common good, open-mindedness, individual responsibility, and negotiation and compromise—that are taught both directly and indirectly so students develop attitudes and values that support civic engagement. This elementary social studies curriculum not only engages students in significant and meaningful questions about our social world, but it also encourages them to think carefully about issues of fairness and ways they can promote justice and the common good.

—————— ✤ ——————

This curriculum not only engages students in significant and meaningful questions about our social world, but it also encourages them to think carefully about issues of fairness and ways they can promote justice and the common good.

Therefore, one core element in providing leadership for teaching social responsibility is realizing that the curricula we select are critical to the development of students' attitudes and skills related to civic engagement. The intellectual involvement, social skill development, and critical thinking promoted by these and other curricular programs provide the foundation for thoughtful participation in the social and political arenas.

SERVICE-LEARNING AND CIVIC ENGAGEMENT

John Dewey believed strongly in learning by doing. An essential component of teaching social responsibility and social justice is connecting young people through meaningful service-learning and civic engagement projects. Service-learning should not be equated with single-event participation in local charitable efforts, such as donating canned goods to the food bank or raising money for a worthy cause. Rather, it is an ongoing activity that is integrally woven into the curriculum, so that it promotes the learning of core concepts and provides a vehicle for authentic assessment of the understanding of those concepts. Also, rather than being a mere afterthought to a unit of study, service-learning is designed into the unit from the outset with clear expectations and outcomes.

There are many excellent examples of high-quality service-learning programs. In Hudson, each grade developed a signature project that was integrated into the curriculum so that students had consistent experiences with service-learning throughout their school years. Kindergartners wrote and laminated math and alphabet books to be sent to children in Uganda as a way of learning essential math and reading skills in addition to social studies concepts. Fourth graders who were studying ecosystems did field research and environmental reclamation work in woodlands and wetlands near their school. Fifth graders were reading buddies for first graders and for special-needs students. Sixth graders studying ancient Greek and Roman cultures staged an educational culture fair for second graders who were also studying cultures from around the world. Ninth graders who were studying civics developed elaborate proposals for service projects that addressed community needs. The potential for excellent service-learning is endless, but what made this approach most effective is that these experiences were deeply inte-grated into the regular curriculum and furthered both curricular and civic engagement goals.

In Jefferson County's social studies curriculum, service-learning is incorporated into each grade as a vehicle for both deeper under-standing and authentic assessment. For example, working closely with

What made this approach most effective is that these experiences were deeply integrated into the regular curriculum and furthered both curricular and civic engagement goals.

Metro United Way, each class of third graders selects one or several organizations in the community that are working to address a community need. They study the work of each organization and the strategies the organization uses to effect change. Classrooms partner with this organization to address directly a specific community need. Building on their research and work with the organization, students sponsor a service fair that educates parents and the public about these organizations, cultivates understanding of the issues these organizations are addressing, and encourages people to volunteer with or donate to the groups. However, the core understanding students derive from this experience is the diversity of strategies that individuals and organizations use to effect change and address community needs within our democratic society.

All too often, service-learning is left to individual teachers who recognize its educational and social value. This results in a scattershot approach of varying quality. To truly provide depth and meaning in service-learning and to promote higher levels of conceptual development of the content, these experiences should be designed collaboratively by teachers and then integrated consistently into the curriculum. In our rush to meet the standards that will be tested, we often forget that depth of understanding is developed experientially rather than through the simple coverage and memorization of material. Service-learning provides that depth through experiences that students long remember.

Service-learning is also key to the development of social responsibility and a sense of social justice. Incremental and consistent experience across school years nurtures an attitude of service and engagement. It provides students with meaning and context for their learning, enabling them to examine social, environmental, and political issues and understand ways that these problems can be addressed. By identifying community needs, issues the community is attempting to address, and issues of injustice, students begin to understand the complexity of the social and political worlds and of finding just solutions to challenging societal problems. They begin to understand that people hold different perspectives on the meaning of social justice in a particular situation. In examining these perspectives, students begin to develop critical reasoning skills, while thinking through which values and viewpoints will afford the greatest benefit to the common good.

PUTTING IT INTO PRACTICE

Leadership is the cumulative effect of many small and large daily decisions. Leadership for social justice and democracy begins with building a sense of community and providing people with a voice in decision making. I have found that the most effective way to start is to engage people in a dialogue about the core values, vision, and mission of the school or district, because in framing this dialogue I can affirm the importance of social responsibility and social justice as central themes that can successfully drive improvement efforts. In Hudson, the expressed core values were empathy, ethics, and service. For Jefferson County, the core values have been framed as teaching for a depth of understanding, meaning, and care. Upon these values, we built our vision and our theory of action that has undergirded all the improvement efforts in the district. In fact, the base that was built, particularly among the key administrative leadership as a result of this dialogue, enabled us to make clear decisions about curriculum, instructional initiatives, and professional development.

However, there are numerous avenues to building a systemic program. Starting small—for example, providing substitutes to enable a few teachers to attend a conference or supporting several teachers who want to integrate service-learning—can also be effective. When I arrived in JCPS, I learned that the district already had successful experience with a social development program entitled the Child Development Program, which was supported by the Developmental Studies Center in Oakland, California. A significant number of teachers who participated in that program had become principals and district leaders. The opportunity to revitalize that program in the form of the CARE for Kids initiative was exciting and renewing, and these leaders threw themselves enthusiastically into building a program that now has the voluntary commitment of almost all the 90 elementary schools and 27 middle schools in the district.

In Hudson, it was service-learning that first captured the interest of teachers and administrators. With a small state grant of $2,000, twenty teachers spent the year exploring service-learning, creating projects for their students, and educating their fellow faculty members. While service-learning began as a "popcorn" approach with many different projects emerging in multiple classrooms, the teacher-leaders began to see the value of building a consistent, well-integrated program across grade levels. Consequently, they designed the "signature" project for each grade that tied deeply into the curriculum. However, they didn't stop there. The teachers soon became interested in exploring social development programs for the classroom that would further students' social skills and sense of social responsibility. As a result, the district implemented Educators for Social Responsibility's Adventures in Peacemaking at the preschool level, the Northeast Foundation for Children's Responsive Classroom, and the Committee for Children's Second Step curriculum at the elementary level, and Origins' Developmental Designs program at the middle school level. Democratic governance even spread to the high school, where teachers not only implemented the Facing History and Ourselves curriculum, but also worked with students to enable young people to experience a greater voice in high school decision making.

My role throughout each of these developmental processes was to encourage, support, and provide opportunities for teachers and administrators, while at the same time raising constructively critical questions as to how the components would blend together into a cohesive and consistent program. The development of the vision, mission, and theory of action paralleled, and was supported by, a growing appreciation for the impact that teaching for social responsibility can have on students and on classroom climate and culture. Each district and school is unique and requires different starting points and strategies, but the role of the leader is invariably key to the ultimate success or failure of the effort. The leader must communicate his or her commitment and support; help guide the growth through focused questions; clear the path by assisting the board, community, and parents to understand and reinforce the effort; and keep an eye on the eventual target of a comprehensive and seamless program that supports both students and staff. The leader also has to help develop a strong understanding of and commitment to this vision among his or her leadership team. The leader cannot be the sole champion. Whether it is an instructional leadership team at a school, a district leadership team in a small district, or a superintendent's cabinet in a large district, the individuals on that team need to be leaders as well.

Often, it is the way we handle the more difficult challenges and decisions that ends up speaking most loudly to a staff. For example, there has been a great deal of focus in Jefferson County on closing the achievement gap between African American students and White students. On deeper examination, however, we discovered that a good deal of this gap was attributable to the students' socioeconomic status. The typical response to achievement gap issues has been to narrow the curriculum for struggling students and to concentrate on the basic skills of reading and math, without ever looking at the underlying causes that might create this gap. Racism and generational poverty leave a long legacy of powerlessness and hopelessness in their wake that significantly impacts children as they grow up. They come to believe that they cannot make a difference in their own lives or in the life of their community. One central element in the achievement gap, then, is an *empowerment* gap—a sense of inability to effect change in one's circumstances and to improve the quality of life within one's community.

Reframing the achievement gap as an empowerment gap enabled us to provide a very different form of intervention that spoke to issues of social justice rather than simply issues of social deprivation.

Reframing the achievement gap as an empowerment gap enabled us to provide a very different form of intervention that spoke to issues of social justice rather than simply issues of social deprivation. It also became clear to administrators and teachers that they could address the empowerment gap through the very curricular programs and school culture and climate initiatives the district was already pursuing. Our CARE for Kids initiative provides students with a sense of safety and community in which they can take classroom-based risks and feel supported. Our work in supporting the cultural competence of our faculty and administrators is enabling our staff to better understand and reach students of different races and ethnic groups. Our social studies curriculum's focus on civics and service will not only give students an understanding of the concepts of community, culture, and civic engagement, but it will also offer them the opportunity to be engaged in service and public policy. Our implementation of inquiry-based math and science curricula provides students with opportunities to openly investigate problems and concepts, think through challenges, and gain deeper levels of understanding. However, the most important aspect of these curricula is that they allow students to take responsibility for their own learning and to gain a sense of empowerment and respect for their abilities.

The key in putting teaching for social responsibility and social justice into practice is the day-to-day coherence among the vision, the directions of the district, and the decisions of key administrators. When these elements are aligned, staff members experience the value and meaning that this work can have for young people and for our future.

LEADERSHIP AND PUBLIC POLICY

All too often, superintendents and other key administrators in a district shy away from advocacy around educational policy because they don't want to appear political or partisan. However, doing so deprives policy makers and the public of valuable lessons we've learned about effective education policy. We also deprive our staff and our students of a model for leadership in the social and political arenas. Whether the issue is charter schools or school funding formulas or accountability systems or student health, leadership for social justice means entering the fray, not as a strident advocate but as a thoughtful and experienced educator who can lend the authority of that experience to public policy decision making.

Influencing policy is a particularly important role for superintendents. Given the leadership we provide on a daily basis and the insight we have gained in struggling with so many educational challenges, it is vital that we help legislators, business leaders, and the community understand the implications of public policy choices. From personal meetings with legislators to op-eds in local newspapers to remarks before chambers of commerce, superintendents can help inform policy makers and the public about the ramifications and opportunities inherent in the public policy choices they are considering.

We also know that advocacy for social justice is more than one individual standing up and voicing a position. Organizations are critical to moving change forward. And so, along with superintendents and other administrators, educational associations can play a critical role through white papers, lobbying, and public information efforts.

OUR FUTURE

Preparing our children to assume a responsible role in the world will be critical to our nation's future welfare, for these young people are inheriting a world replete with significant environmental, political, and social issues. Their ability to discern injustice, understand the complexity of problems, and demonstrate commitment to civic participation is crucial to finding just solutions to those issues. Students, teachers, administrators, superintendents, school board committees, professional associations—all have a part to play in advancing social justice and civic engagement through education. As educators, our duty is doubly momentous, for we serve as role models for the next generation of community leaders, as well as for the average citizen.

Our specific words and deeds may not be long remembered, yet their core-shaping impact will continue to reverberate through the lives of those we teach and lead today. We must ensure that those echoes carry forward the drumbeat of social justice, responsible leadership, and democracy. We would let that message be silenced at our peril.

REFERENCES

Dewey, J. (1897, January). My pedagogic creed. *School Journal, 54,* 77–80.

Dewey, J. (2008). *The middle works of John Dewey, volume 14, 1899 1924: Human nature and conduct, 1922 (Collected works of John Dewey)* (J. Boydston, Ed.). Carbondale: Southern Illinois University Press.

CHAPTER SEVEN

ZERO INDIFFERENCE AND TEACHABLE MOMENTS

SCHOOL LEADERSHIP FOR DIVERSITY, INCLUSION, AND JUSTICE

MARA SAPON-SHEVIN

At South Hadley High School in Massachusetts, Phoebe Prince, recently arrived from Ireland, hung herself in her family's home after ongoing bullying and harassment at her school. Although there is ample evidence that school officials were aware of the harassment (including two visits from Phoebe's mother to talk to teachers and administrators), Phoebe's mother and other parents state that bullying was completely ignored. In March 2010, a Massachusetts state anti-bullying task force was set up as a result of Phoebe's death.

At Itawamba Agricultural High School in Fulton, Mississippi, student Constance McMillen was told that she could not bring her partner, another young woman, to the school prom nor could she wear a tuxedo as she planned. When Constance filed and won a complaint through the ACLU, the school cancelled the prom rather than allow her to attend. The parents, however, did sponsor a different prom—calling it a private party—to which Constance was not invited. Rather, she was informed that the prom would occur elsewhere and she and the special education students were directed to this prom—where they were the only attendees.

At a Michigan high school, a young woman of Arab descent found a death threat in her locker, telling her she would be dead by the end of the day. The school responded strongly with increases in surveillance and attempts to identify the perpetrator through handwriting screening. They did not, however, seize the opportunity to think about what this incident meant for the almost exclusively White school district and what programs of education should be put into place to address anti-Arab and anti-Muslim sentiment in the school. Years earlier in this same school district, the repeated targeting of one of the only African American students in the high school was responded to with disciplinary measures but with no accompanying program to address issues of racial diversity and challenging oppressive behavior. School officials were quoted as saying, "This was an isolated incident. We don't have a problem here."

Brian, a high school student, was repeatedly harassed in his suburban high school. Students tied him up in a volleyball net and threw him in the trash, they ripped his artwork off the walls and urinated on it, and he was shoved in the hallways and taunted with gay epithets. Although Brian talked to school administrators and actually named his attackers, nothing was done. Finally, Brian and his parents were called to the office for a conference during which Brian was told that if he only "stopped acting so gay," the bullying would go away. Nothing happened to his tormentors.

Contrast the above stories with the following, more hopeful possibilities:

At Fayetteville-Manlius High School in New York State, students organized a "Beyond Disabilities" assembly, which stressed the importance of avoiding three hurtful words: retard, moron, and idiot. They held three optional assemblies, which were attended by more than 1,000 students, teachers, and community members. Those who attended were asked to sign the F-M Pledge, which asked that they refrain from using the "R" word and look beyond people's disabilities and recognize their accomplishments. Upon leaving the assembly, each student was given a slip of paper with one of the offending words on it and was asked to shred it in a machine as they passed. The shredding was part of the school's "shred the word to end the word" campaign.

Muslim students observing Ramadan who attend Glen Forest Elementary in Falls Church, Virginia, no longer have to sit in the cafeteria watching their classmates eat when they are fasting. Instead, the school has created a special room filled with toys and games where students can hang out during lunchtime. Gym teachers tell observant children to walk rather than run the mile, and some administrators have postponed festivities or school functions that feature treats until Ramadan ends. All of the students are learning about religious diversity as well as having lessons in respect and thoughtfulness.

At Jamesville-Dewitt High School in New York State, students took part in the annual Day of Silence, a national youth movement in support of lesbian, gay, bisexual, and transgendered (LGBT) individuals. Supporters take an oath of silence for the day to recognize the experiences of LGBT students with discrimination and harassment. Principal Paul Gasparini commended the Acceptance Coalition, which organized the day, for planning an effective event. He said, "The primary mission of a school is to teach democratic participation. These students are truly representing the best form of democratic empowerment."

Last year, nearly 3,000 schools participated in the Mix-It-Up Program, sponsored by Teaching Tolerance of the Southern Poverty Law Center. The program asks students to sit with people at lunch who are outside their usual clique or social group. Although clearly only a beginning, according to Mix It Up at Lunch Day organizers who responded to a 2008 survey conducted by Quality Education Data, the Mix-It-Up program produces powerful results:

- 97% of respondents said students' interactions were positive during Mix It Up at Lunch Day.
- 95% of respondents said Mix It Up at Lunch Day prompted students to interact with people outside of their normal social circles.
- 92% of respondents said Mix It Up at Lunch Day increased awareness about social boundaries and divisions within school.
- 83% of respondents said the event helped students make new friends.
- 79% of respondents said as a result of the Day, students have heightened sensitivity toward tolerance and social justice issues.
- 78% of the respondents said as a result of the Day, students seem more comfortable interacting with different kinds of people.

Source: http://www.tolerance.org/mix-it-up

The differences between these scenarios are stunning but they do *not* contrast schools that have issues of bullying, exclusion, racism, and discrimination and those that do not. Rather, the difference is between schools (and school leaders) who are ignoring (or lamenting) these problems and those that are taking an activist stance; implementing programs; setting and maintaining high standards and expectations; and communicating the critical value of an inclusive, diverse school community.

What does it mean to teach for social justice, and how is it connected to our goals of producing responsible, caring citizens? In an article entitled "Teaching for Social Justice, Diversity, and Citizenship in a Global World," educator James Banks (2004) said that "Citizenship education should help students to develop thoughtful and clarified identifications with their cultural communities, nation-states, and the global community" (p. 289).

Banks (2004) was concerned that when we talk about students' need to develop literacy skills, we neglect the national and global contexts in which they need to be literate. He extended the notion of literacy to "multicultural literacy," arguing that students need

the skills and abilities to identify the creators of knowledge and their interests, to uncover the assumptions of knowledge, to view knowledge from diverse ethnic and cultural perspectives, and to use knowledge to guide action that will create a humane and just world. When we teach students how to critique the injustice in the world, we should help them to formulate possibilities for action to change the world to make it more democratic and just. (p. 291)

In her book *Social Studies for Social Justice,* Rahima Wade (2007) argued that

starting in kindergarten we must educate youth to care about humanity and to begin to understand the immensity of the challenges that will face them as adults. We must embark upon teaching them the skills and knowledge that will ultimately enable them not only to live productive and empowered lives but also to work alongside like-minded others for the betterment of those who suffer from oppression and other inequities. (pp. 1–2)

The lessons we teach our students— whether overtly and intentionally or mindlessly and inadvertently—are what will shape the world they live in.

While some would argue that our responsibility as educators is to prepare students for the wider world, I would argue, instead, that the lessons we teach our students—whether overtly and intentionally or mindlessly and inadvertently—are what will shape the world they live in. Our goal cannot be to mirror the injustices and inequities of the broader society (and world) but rather, to provide students with the skills, attitudes, and confidence they need in order to actively transform the world (Sapon-Shevin, 2007, 2010). Our schools can become sites of justice, inclusion, and caring in which students see and experience new ways of interacting with their peers and increasingly broader communities. We can work to create schools that are models of how we would *like* the world to be.

What would it mean for administrators to set issues of social justice as the center of their leadership? What if school leaders not only recognized their professional and legal responsibilities to create safe schools that model equity and justice, but also realized the tremendous (and exciting) possibilities of leading for social justice? What messages would school leaders hope to communicate to the teachers, parents, and staff at their schools, and how would these be expressed on a daily basis?

This chapter outlines

1. Some of the barriers that impede taking a strong stand in the area of social justice and inclusion;

2. What it would look like if schools put values of social justice and inclusion at the heart of their organizing, programs, and policies.

BARRIERS TO SOCIAL JUSTICE LEADERSHIP

Naming Them and Pushing Them Back

I believe that there are three major barriers to making social justice an organizing priority in schools; by naming these challenges, we may be able to identify ways to respond and to formulate strategies for making our schools powerful beacons of democratic values and places in which students learn to be engaged citizens creating a just world.

1. There's too much to do; administrators are overloaded with managerial and documentation requirements to make social justice a focus.

2. Addressing issues of social justice within the school, including racism, homophobia, classism, poverty, violence, and immigration issues, for example, will be controversial and will divert time and attention from other pressing concerns.

3. Many administrators have received neither training nor support for taking on these issues in their schools. Although they may believe they are important, it is difficult and overwhelming to address all that is included in such a directive.

Without minimizing the reality and power of these barriers, it can be useful to "talk back" to them, both to enhance our own understanding and to develop language that may be useful in articulating the importance of a social justice agenda to others.

Too Much to Do

It is undeniable that teacher-leaders are overburdened and under-supported. The requirements of leading a school include fiscal, administrative, managerial, personnel, and other tasks that can overwhelm and limit administrators' time and focus on broader issues of social justice. Given a conflict between a bus crisis or an out-of-control student and a discussion about how to address racism in the school, it is not surprising that "bigger" issues are often pushed aside in favor of the emergency situation and the immediate concern.

But decisions about how the values of the school are articulated and manifest in the school also happen on a daily basis. It is not a question of what the school's mission statement says (although this can be critical), but about how daily practices and policies represent and model that vision and that mission. Understanding the connection between the bigger vision and responses to day-to-day issues is critical. If there *are* problems in the lunchroom, for example, such as student misbehavior or lack of discipline, this can be seen as an occasion to tighten lunchroom security, hire more lunchroom aides, and seriously curtail students' access and mobility. Or, we could ask different questions regarding how and why students are resisting the regimentation of the lunchroom, to what extent students have been involved in decision making and creative problem solving, and how tensions between different groups of students that have been unaddressed elsewhere are becoming manifest in a more loosely structured social environment. We might, by contrast, do what Sid Morrison, principal of P.S. 84 in New York City, did—organizing the lunch program so that the meal was served "family style," with children sitting at tables together, sharing in serving and cleanup responsibilities. Or, perhaps we would do as they did at Cleeves Primary School in London, setting the lunchroom with tablecloths and flowers, and then finding that students interacted much more politely and maturely.

Failing to address issues of exclusion, diversity, bullying, and violence doesn't mean that they are not present and exacting a toll on staff and students; administrators in schools in which bullying and school violence have reached fatal and well-publicized proportions know that it is a case of "pay now or pay later." There are numerous districts now facing lawsuits in cases where students have committed suicide following ongoing, brutal bullying,

Ongoing, proactive strategies will save time, energy, and sometimes lives.

and schools' staff and leaders are accused of doing too little too late. Ongoing, proactive strategies will save time, energy, and sometimes lives.

"But This Stuff Is Controversial!"

The late activist, educator, and historian Howard Zinn has said that "There's no such place as neutral on a moving train." The poet Dante is quoted as saying, "The hottest places in hell are reserved for those who in times of great moral crises maintained their neutrality." Lastly, the poet and teacher Audre Lorde contributed, "Your silence will not protect you." In contentious educational times such as these, there is no way to remain on the sidelines; failure to take a stand is a powerful message in and of itself.

It is virtually impossible to avoid taking a stand on issues of inclusion/exclusion, diversity, and social justice within schools. Failing to take a stand (like the leaders and teachers who ignored the bullying of Phoebe Prince) means that there is no big vision anchor for smaller decisions. It is impossible to lead from a neutral position. The difference, again, is not between schools that have well-articulated vision and mission statements and those that don't, but between those in which the vision and mission are clearly stated, widely discussed, and constantly negotiated and those in which such conversations are missing or limited, with the predictable effects of inconsistency, confusion, and minimal effectiveness. When racist events happen in a school, for example, and the leaders fail to react or don't act in a strong and powerful way, that nonaction is, in and of itself, a powerful action.

After 11-year-old Jaheem Herrera hanged himself in his bedroom closet, his mother, Masika Bermudez, began planning to sue the DeKalb County School System for alleged negligence. Bermudez says that she complained eight times to officials at Dunaire Elementary School that her son, a fifth grader, was being taunted by bullies who called him "gay" and a "snitch" and who once put him in a sleeper hold in the school bathroom. While avoiding litigation is certainly a powerful motivator for schools, how much better to be proactive in such situations, communicating clear

expectations, addressing bullying
and other ill treatment as if it
really mattered, and implementing effective and ongoing anti-
bullying programs at all levels of
education.

Silence in the face of injustice is a form of collusion.

Federal anti-bullying legislation introduced in 2010 would require schools that receive funding from the Safe and Drug-Free Schools and Communities Act to implement comprehensive anti-bullying policies that define categories targeted by bullies, including race, religion, and sexual orientation. Silence in the face of injustice is a form of collusion.

"I Wasn't Prepared for This!"

In identifying the core requirements for school leadership for social justice, Theoharis (2009) asserted that school leaders must (1) acquire a broad, reconceptualized consciousness/knowledge/ skill base; (2) possess core leadership traits; (3) advance inclusion, access, and opportunity for all; (4) improve the core learning context, both the teaching and curriculum; (5) create a climate of belonging; (6) raise student achievement; and (7) sustain oneself professionally and personally.

Programs that prepare administrators can be evaluated according to the extent that they prepare school leaders to do each of the above. I would argue that item #5, creating a climate of belonging, is key to developing a school climate in which students and teachers can work together for social justice. Unfortunately, a focus on community building is not often privileged in preparing school leaders, although I believe it is antecedent to successful leadership and school change. When Theoharis and I cotaught a course on "Leading the Inclusive School," school administrators were eager for experiences and strategies for community building, noting that such an emphasis had been lacking in their previous preparation. As we implemented weekly opportunities for community building, personal sharing, and peer support in our class, it became clear that although the administrators previously acknowledged these as important for teachers to do in their individual classrooms, it was their responsibility as administrators to create the same kind of safe, inclusive community at a building level.

In an article on preparing inclusive school leaders, Theoharis and Causton-Theoharis (2008) identified three critical dispositions necessary for preparing administrators who are committed to inclusive, socially just schools. The first is that leaders must have a global, theoretical perspective. They must understand that school inclusion is related to other issues of social justice. Issues of racism, homophobia, and other forms of exclusion and marginalization must be at the center of their understanding. Preparation for administrators must include attention to alternatives to tracking, responses to bullying, and the inclusion of all students within a shared school community.

According to Theoharis and Causton-Theoharis (2008), the second critical disposition for leaders of inclusive schools is that they possess a "bold imaginative vision." Educator John Dewey (1916) defined imagination as the capacity to look at things as if they could be different. Although many of our schools are disrupted by violence and are racially segregated, under-resourced, and overburdened, they *could* be different. Educational philosopher Maxine Greene (1999) has added that if you can articulate what *might be,* then you make intolerable *what is.* When we can describe what schools would look like in which students treated one another well, achieved highly, and supported one another's learning, and we work together to address inequities and injustices within the school and in the wider world, then we become increasingly impatient with our current situation.

The third necessary critical disposition is that school leaders "embrace a sense of agency" (Theoharis & Causton-Theoharis, 2008). Leaders must believe that they have the ability to make changes within their schools, that they are not powerless in the face of tremendous challenges. As Henry Ford said, "If you think you can or you can't, you're right." Giving up and giving in are sure signs that things will not change.

CHARACTERISTICS OF SCHOOLS COMMITTED TO SOCIAL JUSTICE

Each of the following can help us think about what our schools could look like and what we would need to get there. For each, consider your own school and identify gaps and inadequacies that can be addressed through bold, creative, visionary leadership.

The School Population Is Purposefully Diverse and Inclusive

Unlike schools in which diversity is seen as a negative characteristic (remember the administrator who reassured me that "Diversity isn't a problem in our school"), in educational settings committed to social justice, student, parent, and staff diversity is regarded as a positive, enriching characteristic of the school. Administrators and teachers regularly (and publicly) celebrate the diversity in their school, and a commitment to multicultural education includes attention to students with disabilities as part of that identity. Students with disabilities are fully included in all classrooms and activities as opposed to there being an "inclusion class," and other forms of tracking are also minimized.

Classrooms are structured in ways that facilitate interactions across groups; practices such as looping, multi-age classrooms, and team teaching model the positive values of diversity and increase the likelihood that students will work with a wider sample of classmates and teachers.

The overrepresentation of students of color in special education and their underrepresentation in high-level and advanced placement classes is seen as highly problematic and the catalyst for curricula and pedagogical reorganization and restructuring efforts in addition to a close study of patterns of counseling and advising.

The School Climate and School Rituals and Practices Reflect a Commitment to Diversity and Inclusion

Every opportunity is used to bring the entire school community together. At Solace Elementary School in Syracuse, New York, every morning begins with a schoolwide assembly and singing. Birthdays are celebrated, accomplishments are acknowledged, and students take responsibility for organizing brief presentations of what they are learning and studying: a play, a song, a skit, and so on.

I often refer to what I call "The Visitor's Test," which asks, What would a visitor to the school discern about the values of the teachers and administrators from entering the building and the classrooms? Whose work is on the walls? How does staff talk to students in the hallways? How do older students relate to younger students? Are parents and other adults evident in the building and in classrooms?

I often refer to what I call "The Visitor's Test," which asks, What would a visitor to the school discern about the values of the teachers and administrators from entering the building and the classrooms?

Joanne Rooney, in an article entitled "School Culture: An Invisible Essential" (2005), described a school in which the principal is closely and warmly connected to his students and staff, and how the school "feels" when you enter it. Rooney described a school's culture as "The way things are done around here," and said, "A school with a wholesome culture knows what it believes in and where it is going." In talking to principals, she tells them that "What their hearts know about school culture is as vital as what their brains know about best practice" (p. 86).

In his article "Measuring School Climate: Let Me Count the Ways," H. Jerome Freiberg (1998) described using three measures (a survey, entrance and exit interviews, and ambient noise checklists) as ways of assessing school climate. In one study, graduating students were asked to respond to the following questions: (1) What do you like about your school? (2) What was your most memorable experience in high school? (3) What would you like to have improved in your school? And (4) What is one message you would like to give your teachers? The data collected provided important information about what students' school experiences were like. Similarly, middle school students were surveyed about what they worried about, providing teachers and administrators with the information they needed to design strategies that would address these concerns.

The Curriculum Reflects a Commitment to Social Justice and Diversity

Schools with a commitment to social justice recognize diversity in the formal curriculum as well. Students are given opportunities to explore both historical and contemporary examples of injustice and resistance to that injustice throughout the curriculum. The school avoids an "additive" or "contributions" approach to multicultural education (Banks, 2004). The contributions of African Americans, for example, are well-integrated in the full curriculum rather than limited to Black History Month in February, and discussions of immigration policy and prejudice and discrimination against Mexican Americans are ongoing.

When diversity and social justice are at the center of the curriculum, students know, for example, that many Native Americans view Columbus Day quite differently than as a day of "discovery and celebration," and are aware that the history presented in their textbooks needs to be analyzed carefully for bias, misrepresentation, and distortion. Students understand why their classmate Noah uses a communication device to express his needs, and they know enough about disability oppression (historical and contemporary) to be aware that not being able to talk is not the same as not having something to say. Students are aware that debates about immigration have direct implications for them and their classmates, and their familiarity with the history of immigration patterns in the United States allows them to frame current debates much more thoughtfully.

The books in the book corner, the posters on the wall, the videos students watch, and every aspect of the physical environment reflect attention to inclusiveness and full representation. Teachers and administrators are alert to the language they use: Letters home are not addressed "Dear Mom and Dad"; teachers refer to the students who are served in the resource room or by the bilingual program with respectful language; and discussions are held to critically examine prejudicial, stereotypical language in the media.

Pedagogical Practices Are Driven and Informed by Social Justice Issues

The curriculum is also taught in ways that acknowledge student diversity and model inclusiveness. Multilevel curriculum units that involve differentiated instruction are designed so that multiple intelligences are honored and represented in what and how students learn. A science unit on walls and bridges, for examples, might become a broader project about how people have used walls and bridges throughout history, including the Great Wall of China, the Wailing Wall in Jerusalem, and the Vietnam War Memorial. The unit might be extended to discuss the ways in which we create walls between ourselves and others and how we can learn to bridge differences to build community and cohesion.

Students are taught how to work with one another in cooperative learning activities that do not simply lump students together in groups, but also pay close attention to how students interact and support one another within those groups. Social skills are taught and monitored to ensure that issues of student status related to gender, race, and ethnicity do not limit the participation of some students (Cohen, 1994). Students engage in peer-tutoring activities and are taught specific skills for supporting and teaching one another. Peer tutoring and peer support cross grade levels as well, so that sixth graders tutor first graders in reading and cross-age projects are implemented—for example, fifth graders designing math games for kindergarteners.

School leaders support differentiated staffing patterns, team teaching, and collaboration by providing planning time and hiring staff who are excited about working in collaborative teams. Patterns of administrative supervision support the maxim that "None of us is as smart as all of us," and staff involvement in teaching decisions is consistent and systematic.

Extracurricular Practices Reflect a Commitment to Diversity and Inclusion

In many schools, patterns of segregation and exclusion extend to after-school and extracurricular activities as well. Particular activities become earmarked for particular groups: You have to be African American to be on the basketball team, only "popular" kids can work on the school paper, the only school choir is reserved for students with really "good" voices, students with disabilities are not welcome in any sports activities, and so on. These activities are also part of a competitive ideology that separates and sorts people according to their putative value. Activities are often designed so narrowly that it becomes difficult to imagine how a nonathletic student could be on the basketball team or how a student who doesn't play a musical instrument could be involved in the band.

Paula Kluth and I (Sapon-Shevin & Kluth, 2003) have written about ways of conceptualizing extracurricular activities inclusively, based on the following four principles: (1) understanding that all students can learn something from participation in extracurricular activities, (2) designing activities in such a way that participation is valued over competition and "winning," (3) believing that participation in extracurricular activities is the right of every learner and not just limited to those who are the "best" in something, and (4) expanding extracurricular options so that the interests and needs of a wider range of students are considered.

When schools offer a wide range of possible groups (e.g., a Salsa dance club, an Anime group, a car repair club, and a quilt-making group), it becomes possible to engage a far greater number of students. Moreover, when these activities are designed and structured so that students can participate at many different skills levels, then the numbers increase further. The school play includes students with disabilities, there are many different music and dance performance groups, and a student with autism manages statistics and record keeping for the basketball team. Extracurricular activities can provide critical opportunities for students to meet and interact with other students they might not associate with during the school day. Crossing boundaries of race, class, gender, ethnicity, language, religion, and dis/ability can result in powerful friendships, increased peer support, and a deeper understanding of and commitment to eliminating prejudice and discrimination.

Zero Indifference, Not Zero Tolerance

A study by the Gay Lesbian Straight Educators' Network (GLSEN, 2005) produced a research report entitled "From Teasing to Torment: School Climate in America." The 2005 study surveyed over 3,400 students aged 13–18 and over 1,000 secondary school teachers, exploring students' and teachers' experiences with bullying and harassment. Among their findings were the following:

- 65% of teens have been verbally or physically harassed or assaulted during the past year because of their perceived or actual appearance, gender, sexual orientation, gender expression, race/ethnicity, disability, or religion.

- 36% of teens indicate that bullying or harassment is a serious problem at their school.
- 53% of secondary school teachers say that bullying or harassment is a serious problem at their school.

Students who are perceived to be LGBT are frequent targets of harassment in school (90% of LGBT teens vs. 62% of non-LGBT teens) and are 3 times as likely as non-LGBT students to not feel safe at school (22% vs. 7%).

The encouraging news from the GLSEN study (2005) is that 73% of teachers strongly agree that they have an obligation to ensure a safe and supportive learning environment for LGBT students. Half of these teachers (47%) believe that antiharassment and antidiscrimination policies would be most helpful in achieving this. Unfortunately, although most schools have some type of antiharassment policy, only about half of these policies specify sexual orientation or gender identity or expression. When policies are more inclusive, they do work; students whose schools have a policy that includes sexual orientation or gender identity/ expression are less likely than other students to report a serious harassment problem at their school (33% vs. 44%), and students from schools with an inclusive policy are also more likely to feel very safe at school (54% vs. 36%), and one-third as likely to skip a class because they felt uncomfortable or unsafe (5% vs. 16%).

Many schools have zero-tolerance policies, meaning that incidents of violence or unacceptable behavior are responded to swiftly and unconditionally with student discipline, including suspension and expulsion. A "zero indifference" policy (a phrase coined by the GLSEN) means something quite different; it means that incidents of bullying, harassment, discrimination, and prejudice are taken seriously and responded to consistently. Although the "solutions" may be multilayered and ongoing, students and teachers know that schools take discriminatory behavior seriously and will respond.

A zero indifference policy means . . . that incidents of bullying, harassment, discrimination, and prejudice are taken seriously and responded to consistently.

What can administrators do? The 2007 National School Climate Survey (GLSEN, 2008), which surveyed over 6,000 LGBT students in Grades K–12, found that students in schools with a Gay–Straight

Alliance reported hearing fewer homophobic remarks and experienced less harassment and assault because of their sexual orientation, were more likely to report incidents of harassment and assault, were less likely to feel unsafe because of their sexual orientation or gender expression, were less likely to miss school because of safety concerns, and reported a greater sense of belonging to their school community.

Students from schools with a comprehensive, enumerated policy reported a less hostile and more supportive school climate; heard fewer homophobic remarks; were more likely to report incidents of harassment and assault; and reported that school staff intervened most of the time or always when hearing homophobic language in school (29.1%), compared to students in schools with generic policies (17.5%) or no policies (13.1%; GLSEN, 2008).

These statistics provide compelling evidence that problems of bullying and harassment are not limited to particular groups and that solving the problem involves a whole-school, comprehensive approach. This is not a zero-sum situation; eliminating any kind of bullying has a positive effect on overall school climate.

Students in the Hermitage School District in Pennsylvania are asked to sign the "Stop the Sting of Bullying" pledge, which applies not only inside the school but also on the school grounds and on school buses. Students agree to do the following:

- Treat others respectfully
- Try to include those who are left out
- Refuse to bully others
- Refuse to watch, laugh, or join in when someone is being bullied
- Tell an adult
- Help those who are being bullied (Harrison, 2005)

What is interesting about this pledge is the understanding that being a bystander is as significant as bullying and that exclusion is a form of bullying.

Unfortunately, it is not just the behavior of students that must be closely monitored and responded to forcefully and clearly. At Jesse Bethel High School in Vallejo, California, it was teachers and staff members who daily ridiculed Rochelle Harrison who has been openly gay since age 13. They taunted her with assaults of "You'll never get a job," "You're going to hell," and "You're so ignorant. You don't even know whether you're a boy or a girl." Although Harrison's mom, Cheri, wrote letters, made phone calls, and scheduled meetings with school officials, the harassment continued, and so the Harrisons finally turned to the ACLU for support. After a year of effort, Harrison was awarded $25,000, which will go into a trust fund. The school district was also required to write and adopt a policy prohibiting discrimination based on sexual orientation and gender identity. All students and teachers will be required to receive mandatory antiharassment training (Maxwell, 2009).

Teachable Moments for Social Justice Are Seized, Not Ignored

When things happen that violate the school's vision of inclusiveness and respect for diversity, the response is educational rather than punitive. In the incident described earlier in which an Arab-American student received repeated death threats, in addition to trying to apprehend the culprit(s) and improve security measures, the school would immediately have asked the following questions of themselves and their staff: (a) What do our students, parents, and staff know about Arab Americans and what misconceptions might be in place? (b) How are Arab-American students and parents in our school treated and how will we find out? (c) What steps can we take now and in the future to ensure that all students, including Arab-American students, feel welcomed and safe in school and that all staff are attentive, alert, and responsive to incidents of prejudice or ill treatment?

In the wake of recent anti-immigration legislation in Arizona and California, students at Live Oak High School in Morgan Hill, California, chose May 5th (Cinco de Mayo) to make statements about issues of nationality and pride by wearing American flag T-shirts at the same time that some of their classmates were wearing shirts in the colors of the Mexican flag (red, white, and green). The principal, Miguel Rodriguez, called the shirts "incendiary," and, fearing a fight, required the boys to either remove their American flag t-shirts or turn them inside out. As Leonard Pitts, Jr. (2010), a columnist for the *Miami Herald,* reported, it was the decision to send some of the boys home that became incendiary.

The case certainly raises issues of First Amendment rights (and the infringement thereof), but as Pitts (2010) pointed out, this educator missed a teachable moment. He wrote,

> Imagine if Rodriguez had corralled the most articulate of the T-shirt boys and the Cinco de Mayo celebrators and required them to research and represent their points of view in a formal debate before the entire school. The T-shirt kid could have challenged his classmates to explain why he felt the need, if he is an American, to celebrate a foreign holiday. The classmate could have pressed the T-shirt kid on why he felt threatened by a simple acknowledgment of heritage and cultural origin. (p. A16)

There is no shortage of teachable moments about diversity and social justice. Following the passage of a harsh anti-immigrant law by the state legislature in Arizona, the school district in Prescott, Arizona, found themselves embroiled in a controversy.

Miller Valley Elementary School had hired a muralist to celebrate their "Go Green" campaign, and the mural featured the faces of four Latino students who attend the school. Following the passage of the anti-immigration bill, however, a city councilman and radio personality named Steve Blair complained about the brown skin of the depicted faces, and passing motorists yelled racial slurs as they drove by the school.

The school district's first response was to ask the muralist to "lighten" the faces of the children on the mural, but this decision was met with a fierce outcry and protests. Soon thereafter, principal Jeff Lane mounted the scaffold adjacent to the mural and announced that he had made a mistake and asked the muralist to restore the original color to the faces of the students on the mural. He was joined by School Superintendent Kevin Knapp who said, "It is okay that this issue has become a major issue. Prescott is truly my home town, and it's good for the town to stand up once in a while and take a look at itself, and this mural has done that" (Cody, 2010, n.p.).

In telling the story of the Prescott mural debacle, journalist Anthony Cody (2010) shared the following contrastive story in an article entitled "Arizona Mural Teaches a Lesson About Racism":

On Friday I attended my nephew's high school graduation in Healdsburg, California. Healdsburg is a small town in Sonoma County, and the student body seemed to be about half Latino, and half white. The principal, John Curry, spoke about how the school had embraced a commitment to being inclusive through their participation in the Challenge Day process. The national anthem was sung by a Latina, who later delivered a five minute–long speech entirely in Spanish. Hearing this young woman speak her language sent a powerful message. It honored the Spanish-speaking parents and grandparents by expressing to them what the occasion meant to the students. It also explicitly honored the language and culture of the Latino students at the school.

Clearly, school leadership can make a huge difference in how students, parents, and teachers understand issues of diversity, civil rights, inclusion, and social justice.

Students and Their Parents
Have Active Roles in the School

It is impossible to lead a school committed to social justice if the entire school community is not involved in the process. Students must feel that their voices are truly heard; there should be student representatives on most school committees, and clear ways for students to communicate issues and concerns to administrators. Parents must have similar access to the school and to schoolwide decision making. Parental involvement cannot be limited to the bake sale and chaperoning field trips.

On Friday, June 4, 2010, following announced school budget cuts in New York City, about 30 teachers, parents, and students participated in a protest in front of P.S. 197. Signs read "No more budget cuts!" "Charters bribe; public schools teach!" "Parents-teachers united will never be defeated!" "Children first, no cuts in education!" "Hands off teachers! No to layoffs!" This was a true collaboration between parents and teachers who were supporting their public school against what they saw as devastating budget cuts, a focus on high-stakes testing rather than education, and real threats to teachers' decision making and professionalism.

Critical issues such as bullying (particularly cyber-bullying), multicultural education and culturally relevant pedagogy, and tracking and inclusion issues affect the entire community and cannot be effectively addressed without the involvement of parents and guardians. If a child bullies in schools and then is told by parents that "it's no big deal," or "that kid deserved it," it will be difficult to implement whole-school systemic reform.

Teachers Are Well-Supported for Addressing Social Justice Issues

When teachers tackle challenging issues of social justice and inclusion through their curriculum or their classroom policies and practices, they need to know they will have administrative support. A teacher came to me in tears recently. After repeated instances of racial bullying on the playground, she had gone to the principal seeking support for implementing programming and educational activities to support anti-oppressive education with her students. She was informed that the upcoming high-stakes testing had to take precedence and that there simply "wasn't time for that stuff." The teacher's attempts to explain the relationship between the atmosphere of bullying and exclusion and students' abilities to learn (and do well on tests) was seen as interesting but not compelling.

At another school, a third-grade teacher showed a video about families that depicted step families, multiracial families, adoptive and foster care families, single parents, and gay and lesbian parents. The teacher was chastised for her behavior and told that she had no right to make independent decisions about controversial issues such as family diversity. Although the video was shown as part of a unit on families and diversity, there was no support for the importance of teaching that all children and their families are welcomed in the school.

Teachers must have clear channels of communication with and support from administrators as they attempt to deal with challenging issues in their classrooms and the schools. In one case, a teacher's concern about conflict on the playground led to the implementation of a schoolwide peer mediation program with excellent results. Teachers are generally finely attuned to the needs and situations of their students, and they must have administrative support for their efforts to address difficult (even controversial) issues within their pedagogical and curricular framework.

In an article about school culture, Peterson and Deal (1998) described schools that have toxic cultures, particularly among teachers. They described a high school in which "disgruntled staff came to faculty meetings ready to attack new ideas, criticize those teachers concerned about student achievement, and make fun of any staff member who volunteered to go to conferences or workshops" (p. 28). Peterson and Deal argued that leaders must be able to "read the culture" of the school and then attempt to "fashion a positive context" through good communication, honoring and recognizing (I would argue not competitively) those who are making progress and observing rituals and traditions that support a positive school culture. One principal I know gives awards not only for exciting projects, but also for "great ideas that didn't work," thus honoring courage and initiative and not just achievement.

Administrators Seek and Structure Ongoing Support for Themselves

The preceding nine items are of gigantic proportions. It is easy to be overwhelmed, and public criticism often abounds. School leaders must find ways to support one another in their goals and challenges. Monthly (if not weekly) meetings of small groups of administrators who get together to share successes and problems can be invaluable in combating isolation and hopelessness. In addition, given the ongoing changes in research and policies related to education, attendance at workshops, conferences, and other professional development opportunities enhances access to cutting-edge developments. At a professional conference I attended on full inclusion, several teams presented about what had been implemented at their school; each team consisted of an administrator and several teachers. The shared learning, sense of accomplishment, and camaraderie was evident, and it was clear that they were supporting one another in a shared enterprise.

On my wall hangs a painting by Ann Altman with a quote from Diane Ackerman that reads, "I swear I will not dishonor my soul with hatred, but offer myself humbly as a guardian of nature, as a healer of misery, as a messenger of wonder, as an architect of peace." We can weigh each decision, each policy, each public stance, and each silence against a rubric of social justice: Will what I am doing here and now move us forward toward creating equity, social justice, and inclusion, or farther away? Let us support ourselves and one another in becoming school leaders who use our power and positions to create a world fit for us all and schools that prepare students to be actively engaged in that process.

REFERENCES

Banks, J. (2004, Summer). Teaching for social justice, diversity and citizenship in a global world. *The Educational Forum, 68,* 289–298.

Cody, A. (2010). *Arizona mural teaches a lesson in racism.* Retrieved June 10, 2010, from http://blogs.edweek.org/teachers/living-in-dialogue/2010/06/arizona_mural_teaches_a_lesson.html

Cohen, E. (1994). *Designing groupwork: Strategies for the heterogeneous classroom* (2nd ed.). New York: Teachers College Press.

Dewey, J. (1916). *Democracy and education.* New York: Macmillan.

Freiberg, H. J. (1998). Measuring school climate: Let me count the ways. *Educational Leadership, 56*(1), 22–26.

GLSEN. (2005, October 11). *From teasing to torment: School climate in America—A national report on school bullying.* Retrieved June 10, 2010, from http://www.glsen.org/cgi-bin/iowa/all/library/record/1859.html?state=research&type=research

GLSEN. (2008, October 8). *2007 National School Climate Survey.* Retrieved June 10, 2010, from http://www.glsen.org/cgi-bin/iowa/all/library/record/2340.html?state=research&type=research

Greene, M. (1999, February 13). *Presentation to the North Dakota Study Group,* Chicago.

Harrison, M. M. (2005, Fall). Bully on the bus. *Teaching Tolerance, 28,* 38–43.

Maxwell, L. (2009, May 19). Openly gay student wins lawsuit. *News.* Retrieved November 19, 2010, from http://sfist.com/2009/05/19/openly_gay_student_wins_lawsuit.php

Peterson, K. D., & Deal, T. E. (1998). How leaders influence the culture of schools. *Educational Leadership, 56*(1), 28–30.

Pitts, L., Jr. (2010, May 19). A teachable moment lost. *The (Syracuse) Post-Standard,* p. A16.

Rooney, J. (2005, February). School culture: An invisible essential. *Educational Leadership, 62*(5), 86.

Sapon-Shevin, M. (2000/2001). Schools fit for all. *Educational Leadership,* 5–10.

Sapon-Shevin, M. (2007). *Widening the circle: The power of inclusive classrooms.* Boston: Beacon Press.

Sapon-Shevin, M. (2010). *Because we can change the world: A practical guide to building cooperative, inclusive classroom communities* (2nd ed.). Thousand Oaks, CA: Corwin.

Sapon-Shevin, M., & Kluth, P. (2003). In the pool, on the stage, and at the concert: Academics beyond classroom walls. In P. Kluth, D. Straut, & D. Biklen (Eds.), *Access to academics* (pp. 167–184). Mahwah, NJ: Lawrence Erlbaum.

Theoharis, G. (2009). *The school leaders our children deserve: Seven keys to equity, social justice, and school reform.* New York: Teachers College Press.

Theoharis, G., & Causton-Theoharis, J. N. (2008). Oppressors of emancipators: Critical dispositions for preparing inclusive schools leaders. *Equity and Excellence in Education, 41*(2), 230–246.

Wade, R. (2007). *Social studies for social justice: Teaching strategies for the elementary classroom.* New York: Teachers College Press.

CHAPTER EIGHT

GETTING KIDS READY FOR SCHOOL—RAISING THE VILLAGE

PAUL D. HOUSTON

> How are the children?
>
> —Masai greeting

When I was superintendent in Tucson, we had a governor who was impeached. He was followed by a governor who was sent to prison, making Arizona a state for the gubernatorially challenged. The one who was impeached brought a man who had been in the state legislature into his office to be his education adviser. He had only completed the eighth grade and had been a longtime advocate for "creationism" in schools—making him the

Source: From Houston, P. (2010). *Giving Wings to Children's Dreams: Making Our Schools Worthy of Our Children,* Chapter 8. Thousand Oaks, CA: Corwin. Reprinted with permission.

perfect education adviser, I suppose. Because he could no longer introduce his creationism bill, he had a friend do so, but he testified on its behalf. In his testimony, he said that schools have no right to teach anything parents don't want taught. One of the legislators asked, "Do you mean that if the parents think the Earth is flat, the school has no right to teach them differently?" He said, "Absolutely." Of course, the next day the papers were buzzing about the governor's education man who thought the Earth was flat.

That day, a reporter came to see me and asked what I thought about the "flat Earth" situation. I was in one of those playful moods that screamed, "Not a good day to talk to the press," but there she was, so I said, "I'm very concerned. I have 60,000 kids I'm responsible for. What happens if one of them walks over to the edge and falls off? I have safety issues to consider and liability questions to think about. This is serious!"

She said, "Now, do you really think that the Earth is flat?"

I opened the drapes to my window and pointed out to the sidewalk and parking lot. "Look at that. I don't know why I never noticed it before."

Continuing the tongue-in-cheek dialogue, or in my case the foot-in-mouth responses, she asked me the question all superintendents get on a daily basis: "What are you going to do about it?" I told her that I had given it some thought. I was going to ask the community for donations of parachutes. That way we could equip the children with them, and if they fell off the edge, they could just pull their ripcords and float down.

She asked me if she could get a picture of me standing in front of a globe. I told her that I had sent all the globes to the warehouse to have them flattened and we didn't have any in the office. The next day, the front page of the paper had a headline, "Houston Fears for Student Safety." My friends got me a T-shirt that said, "Get Your Chute Together."

This is a true story that, among other things, demonstrates the danger of talking to the press when you are in a playful mood. But it also shows the kinds of controversies schools get into on topics that have no educational value. It depicts the expectations that no matter what the problem, the school leader is expected to "do something" about it. It also shows the willingness I had as a superintendent to engage the community in solving problems my students faced, which is really the only way school problems can truly be handled.

There is a famous African proverb that educators love to quote: "It takes a village to raise a child." This strikes at the heart of the challenge for educators. The task of educating can only be done successfully if there is a team working on the challenge. Schools are tasked with the central mission of educating—that is why parents send their children off each morning. But education does not take place in a vacuum. If the child is sick, abused, or ill prepared, the school is rolling the rock uphill in trying to overcome these issues. It takes parents and the broader community to help. But often in today's world, those elements are missing. So when educators want to quote the proverb, they need to ask a follow-up question: "What does it take to raise a village?" In modern society, the village is as antiquated as stagecoaches and buggy whips. Children are growing up today in a world lacking in the web of support that is necessary for success.

That means the first task of a school is to shoulder the burden of remaking the village. This is the only way real success is possible. But schools also exist at the physical and psychological center of communities. If you walk through most communities, it won't take you long to find a school. Historically, most communities were either built around a school or the school was placed in the center of the community. Initially, that was so children could walk to school. As communities grew, or desegregation plans were undertaken, it meant that children would be bused to school, but the "centeredness" of the school prevails to this day. Also, the school is often the place where other activities occur. In the case of older children, the music and drama productions and the sports programs draw the community to the school. So the school has been at the physical center of communities, and it has also occupied the social and psychological center. Although society has changed, the school is still there, and it could be used as a magnet for creating a more vibrant village. But often, schools have not taken full advantage of that central location. Historically, educators viewed their work as *their* work, and the community was kept at arm's length. That has started changing, but most schools are still not using their centrality as a means of creating a stronger community. How might they do that, and what should be happening?

First and foremost, school folks need to help bring people together. I used to have a little joke sign in my office that said, "The time for action is past, and now is the time for senseless bickering." I finally put the sign away because so many communities are caught up in all sorts of controversy, and they need no encouragement to do senseless bickering. From fights over books in the library or curriculum to differences over coaches or who made the cheerleading squad, there are far too many adult agendas being played out around the school. It would be good to remember the less well-known African proverb that speaks beautifully to this: "When the elephants fight, the grass gets trampled." In today's world, we have far too many children being trampled because the focus is on the adults rather than the children. Being a school person in today's world requires that you be a peacemaker. The first step toward creating a village is raising the awareness of everyone that the children are the central client and that adult agendas undermine that crucial work. We need a sign that quotes the infamous Rodney King: "Can't we all just get along?"

Being a school person in today's world requires that you be a peacemaker. The first step toward creating a village is raising the awareness of everyone that the children are the central client and that adult agendas undermine that crucial work.

School people are often the biggest culprits in these battles. I have sat in far too many faculty meetings and through too many school board meetings where every item on the agenda was centered on adult concerns: teaching schedules, lunchroom duty, teacher contracts, staff hiring or firing, and so on. Although many of these things need to be addressed, when they become the center of the work, then something very important is getting lost—a focus on children. So when it comes to creating a community, educators must start with the notion from medicine: "Physician, heal thyself." Peacemaking starts in the school. From there, it is much easier to bring parents and the broader community in and help them work together.

My reputation as a superintendent was as a "healer." When I arrived in one particular community known for its epic battles over the schools, a television interviewer laid out a long litany of controversies in the community and asked me the "gotcha" question, "How are you going to heal this mess?" My answer was simple: "My job isn't to heal the problems here. My job is to create the conditions so that the community can heal itself." School leaders must be in the "healership" business. That simply means, don't be the source of the conflict, and work to allow the people who care most about the schools—the parents and community—to find ways to work together for the benefit of the children.

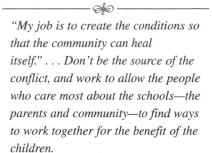

"My job is to create the conditions so that the community can heal itself." . . . Don't be the source of the conflict, and work to allow the people who care most about the schools—the parents and community—to find ways to work together for the benefit of the children.

That leads naturally to the next step—opening up the school to the broader community. First, we must make schools more parent friendly. Schools should do periodic checks on how friendly they are. One idea used by some is to do an annual customer survey that asks people a series of questions around this issue. Community checkups are revealing and give a great sense of what the school can do to bring the community closer. The mere act of asking their opinions even creates a more positive feeling for the school.

I have known some principals or superintendents to have a friend, not known to the staff, come to the office to see how they are treated. In today's post-Columbine world, schools have, by necessity, closed in to protect children from possible harm. But some schools have been able to do this without creating a fortress-like environment. I have sometimes joked that rather than doing school reform, we are doing *reform school* (metal detectors, uniforms, and guards). If a school looks a lot like a prison and feels like a prison, the students will begin to act like prisoners.

A superintendent friend of mine told me that in his former district, the school board bought plans for a prison and used them to build their high school. They saved some money on architecture fees, but I have no idea what that communicated to the community and what it cost them in creating a learning environment that was welcoming, but I can imagine what it said to the students. It is doubtful that we have really made the children that much safer, and by creating a prison-like atmosphere, we have done terrible damage to the work that should be going on in schools. We should not create schools as places where parents feel like they are going for visitation or where we are fearful of their bringing in a hacksaw hidden in the cupcakes so they can break out their children. One simple thought would be to create a school environment that we would want for our children and one where we would feel welcomed.

For parents, I strongly believe we need to go further. It is not just a matter of making them feel welcomed. It is a matter of using their natural interest in their children to enhance the learning environment and help them be more effective parents. I have always found it amusing that we give students driver's education training but we don't give them *parent* education training, which is a much more complex and important role. We should make certain that in the middle or high school curriculum or in the health classes that most schools require, a portion is dedicated to basic parent training. They should be given a basic understanding of child development and ways parents can work with children to help them learn. For many students, this is something they will need down the road, but for too many, it is something they will use too soon, as teenagers are having children often before they graduate.

I also think schools should provide training for current parents. In several of the districts where I worked, we created a Parent Academy that offered classes in dealing with such things as understanding your teenager and sibling rivalry. These classes were welcomed by the parents and bonded the district to the parents. Parents were eager for the support, and the school benefited by having parents who were better at their jobs, which naturally made our job easier. In Riverside, California, we went so far as to have a class for African American parents that helped them understand the unique challenges faced by their children. It was one of the most popular classes we held. Let me be clear: Most parents want to be successful parents and want their children to succeed, and most parents could benefit from a better understanding of how to be more effective in their role. If some parents request help, as the African American parents in Riverside did, we should try to help them.

It is particularly important to help low-income parents understand what they can do to help their children be more effective in school. They want to help, but they are often overwhelmed by circumstances, and the school can help. Study after study has shown that the home environment is critical to student success. One of the most significant predictors of students' SAT scores is their parents' wealth: the richer the parent, the higher the score tends to be. I used to joke that if district leaders wanted to raise SAT scores, all they needed to do was get their children born into wealthier families. Well, obviously, that is not a plan that will work. This is also a very serious indictment of a class-based system, which we still have in the United States. The students we work with are born to those they were born to. But we can look at what it is that makes children of wealthy parents more successful and give those insights to the parents who are less fortunate. But it is important not to just assume low-income parents have problems. When I was in Princeton, New Jersey, a very wealthy community, we found many children were "psychologically abandoned" by parents who were too busy with their careers and lives to help their children. Child rearing in America is a major issue, and to the extent that schools can better support more effective child rearing, they should.

But social class still underpins many educational issues. There have been studies conducted on parent language—how many words an hour parents speak to their children. One study by Betty Hart and Todd Risley (2003) at the University of Kansas showed that, on average, professional parents speak 2,000 words an hour to their children, while working-class parents speak 1,300 words an hour, and low-income mothers speak 600 words an hour. This means that by age 3, children of professional parents have a vocabulary 50% greater than working-class children and 200% greater than low-income children. Other studies have looked at the kinds of words parents speak to children. Are they reprimanding or encouraging? Again, middle-class parents significantly use more encouraging language while lower-income parents use more reprimand. Because children from middle- and upper-middle-class homes have many more words spoken to them than those of low-income homes and they receive many more encouraging words than reprimands than low-income children, it should be no surprise that this impacts student achievement.

Giving low-income parents this awareness and showing what they can do to help their children could have a significant impact on later achievement. A small change could come from them taking their children to the supermarket, and then, instead of telling the children to keep their hands off everything, the parent talks to them about what they are doing and ask the children questions about what they are seeing. This will build language and vocabulary. We cannot take children who have had 4 or 5 years of limited language development and expect that they will be successful in school. But we can begin to intervene in those first 5 years to start to change the arc of their lives by helping their parents do a great job as the child's first teacher. However, to do so requires that schools rethink their organization and philosophy to make certain that parents are central in that thinking.

Certainly, the issue of early childhood education is also central to all this. Many of the developed countries, as a matter of course, enter children in formal schooling at age 3 and provide quality day care even earlier. In America, our day care is a patchwork of solutions, some good and some pretty awful—and that is just for those who can access day care. The research that grew out of the Perry Preschool program (Schweinhart, 1994), years ago, showing that students who have been in Head Start programs benefit for years, should be no surprise, but it hasn't had much impact on policy at the state or national level. The point here is that giving children experiences that stimulate them and offering them opportunities for vocabulary development that affirms them would have tremendous payoffs for them and for the country.

But engaging parents and offering early learning experiences is not enough. Schools must find ways of getting the whole community involved in the education of children. In most communities, only about 30% of the population has children in school. The rest have either already raised their children or do not have children. This is a critical issue for schools as they try to pass budget or bond votes—you are talking to people who feel they do not have a dog in the fight and who care much less about what happens to children. The attitude from this segment of the population is often either "it's not my problem" or "I raised my kids; now it's someone else's problem." So, if for no other reason than the most practical, schools must reach out to the community. But the community can play a much larger part—they can help educate children.

With the graying of the baby boomers, there are increasing numbers of people who are retired and underutilized. They have much to offer. The creation of volunteer and tutoring programs can draw on this valuable resource. Study after study shows that if a child feels connected, he or she does better. Being connected to a caring adult can make all the difference for many children. A core human need is having a sense of purpose. Making it easy for members of the community to contribute to the future of children is a very powerful purpose, and it gives the children, many of whom come from homes where the support is often not available, the scaffolding to become stronger.

It is also clear that we live in a society that segregates our population by age. Most non-parenting adults have little contact with children. Because of our mobile society, most children today do not live near their grandparents and have little contact with older people. Finding ways to bring adults into schools helps offset this. Schools, rather than trying to keep non-parents out, should find ways of bringing them into the building. In the district I led in Princeton, we opened our cafeteria to the adults in the community. It helped our food service bottom line, it helped some of the elderly in the community who were on fixed incomes (and made them like us a lot more), and it put students in contact with a different generation. We also opened classes that had excess seats to adults. I once walked into a class that was studying World War II that had a "community student" there who had actually *fought* in World War II. Imagine the lively discussion I was able to hear—talk about living history! There are hundreds of ways to connect the schools to the community. We are limited only by our imagination and our courage to step out of the commonly accepted ideas of what schools should look like.

One of the key ways of involving community with school is through the creation of *community*

> We opened classes . . . to adults. I once walked into a class that was studying World War II that had a "community student" there who had actually fought in World War II. Imagine the lively discussion I was able to hear!

schools. These are places where not only are courses offered to the community, but also the resources of the community are brought in to serve the children. A school I had in Riverside, California, set up a clinic where doctors and dentists had regular visits to service children at the school, but they also serviced the low-income parents who needed help. The school also had resident social workers from some of the community organizations who found it much easier to gain access to students and their families by being in the school rather than trying to get them to come to their locations. We even had a branch of the welfare office there so parents didn't have to go downtown to get service. New York City has had a long-standing relationship with the Children's Aid Society, which has done great work in bringing support resources from the community into the school in a number of settings. The point is that there are many ways to get this done, but it has to start with a sense of openness from the school to get things moving.

One of the major ways schools can work with the community is in the area of after-school activities. Not only should school facilities be made available to the community, but the community can also support the needs of the school in the after-school area. After we were able to pass a bond in Princeton to upgrade our athletic facilities, we welcomed the community to use them when they were not being used by students. We had community members playing ball on our fields and jogging on our track. It made the next bond a lot easier to pass because people saw that they benefited, too.

Giving parents and other community members access to facilities opens up possibilities for them and makes it easier on the children. You can also provide more enrichment activities by inviting the community to share their expertise with students. We had mothers who had no formal education but who could cook or do crafts, leading classes on those things they were good at. In the low-income areas, this had the added bonus of letting the parents and students

We had mothers who had no formal education but who could cook or do crafts, leading classes on those things they were good at. In the low-income areas, this had the added bonus of letting the parents and students know that we valued what they and their families were bringing to the school.

know that we valued what they and their families were bringing to the school.

You can also benefit the staff with more community involvement. In Princeton, we had an annual symposium where we invited members of the community who were doing interesting work to share it with our staff. Because we were very rich in community intellectual capital, we had professors and researchers to draw from. A community less endowed on this front might be able to use small-business people or farmers to bring insight to the staff. The point here is that the staff learns something, and the community walks away with a deeper appreciation of its teaching force. It is a win–win situation.

To do any of this village raising requires a new attitude from school leaders. I have often suggested that we should stop talking about superintendents of schools or principals of schools and start talking about superintendents or principals of *learning*. It is not about the place as an isolated venue but about the processes and the relationships. We have to see leaders worry less about the killer *B*s of leadership—buildings, buses, books, bonds, budgets—and begin to be become master of the *C*s—communication, community building, collaboration, and connection. It is about understanding that learning is a 24/7 proposition. The school plays an important role as facilitator, but to truly make a difference in the lives of children, the whole 360 degrees of their existence must be taken into consideration. Getting children ready for school means starting to think about what needs to happen at the prenatal level and how the schools might have an impact on that. It means finding ways to see that children's health needs are met while they are toddlers and what the school can do to facilitate that. It means finding ways to help parents parent effectively. It means finding ways of bringing the school and community together to make a difference in the lives of children. We know that much of the child's critical learning takes place well before he or she gets to school. We must find ways of intervening in those years so that positive results can ensue. We also know that about 90% of a child's life is spent outside of school, and we have to create ways of working with parents and the community to see that those hours are not wasted. This is raising the village and putting parachutes on the children, so when they fall down, they won't get hurt.

REFERENCES

Hart, B., & Risley, T. (2003). The early catastrophe: The 30 million word gap by age 3. *American Educator, 27*(1). Retrieved November 12, 2010, from http://archive.aft.org/pubs-reports/american_educator/spring2003/catastrophe.html

Schweinhart, L. J. (1994). *The lasting benefits of preschool programs.* Urbana, IL: ERIC Clearinghouse on Elementary and Early Childhood Education. (ERIC Identifier: ED365478)

INDEX

CORWIN
A SAGE Company

The Corwin logo—a raven striding across an open book—represents the union of courage and learning. Corwin is committed to improving education for all learners by publishing books and other professional development resources for those serving the field of PreK–12 education. By providing practical, hands-on materials, Corwin continues to carry out the promise of its motto: **"Helping Educators Do Their Work Better."**

The HOPE Foundation logo stands for Harnessing Optimism and Potential Through Education. The HOPE Foundation helps to develop and support educational leaders over time at district- and state-wide levels to create school cultures that sustain all students' achievement, especially low-performing students.

American Association of
School Administrators

The American Association of School Administrators, founded in 1865, is the professional organization for over 13,000 educational leaders across America. AASA's mission is to support and develop effective school system leaders who are dedicated to the highest quality public education for all children.